HEAVEN
My Father's Country

Books by Ivor Powell

Bible Cameos
Bible Gems
Bible Highways
Bible Names of Christ
Bible Nuggets
Bible Oases
Bible Pinnacles
Bible Promises
Bible Windows
Matthew's Majestic Gospel
Mark's Superb Gospel
Luke's Thrilling Gospel
John's Wonderful Gospel
The Amazing Acts
The Exciting Epistle to the Ephesians
David: His Life and Times
Heaven: My Father's Country
What in the World Will Happen Next?

HEAVEN
My Father's Country

Ivor Powell

kregel
PUBLICATIONS

Grand Rapids, MI 49501

Heaven: My Father's Country by Ivor Powell.

Copyright © 1995 by Kregel Publications, a division of Kregel, Inc., P. O. Box 2607, Grand Rapids, MI 49501. Kregel Publications provides trusted, biblical publications for Christian growth and service. Your comments and suggestions are valued.

Cover Photograph: Ron Lowery / THE STOCK MARKET
Cover and Book Design: Alan G. Hartman

Library of Congress Cataloging-in-Publication Data
Powell, Ivor, 1910–
    Heaven: my Father's country / Ivor Powell.
    p. cm.
    Includes bibliographical references.
    1. Heaven—Christianity. I. Title.
BT846.2.P68   1995   236'.24—dc20   95-8339
                                               CIP

ISBN 0-8254-3517-X (paperback)

2 3 4 5 Printing / Year 99 98

Printed in the United States of America

Contents

Introduction

It is a remarkable fact that few people know anything about heaven. Throughout the history of the church, preachers have spoken about hell and other doctrines of the Bible, but they have not been eloquent in explaining what may be found in God's country. The fact that most people believe such a place exists has helped clergymen to comfort bereaved relatives. It has been rewarding to assure families that their departed loved ones have gone to be with God. Emotional evangelists have spoken of the reality of hell, but some failed to give equal time to other subjects. It is a mistake to speak of what might be lost in eternity if what might be gained in heaven is omitted from the message.

At the age of eighty-three I asked myself what I knew about the home of God, and I was truly shocked to admit I knew very little. Increasing age emphasized mortality. Man's sojourn upon earth is strictly limited and uncertain; wise travelers make preparation for the inevitable. People who plan foreign vacations visit travel agents, consult brochures, plan the journey, obtain a passport, and attend to details that ordinarily would never be considered. The best brochure about eternity is the Bible. Yet because people are too busy to read the Scriptures, they remain ignorant of details they urgently need to know. Where is heaven? What can be known about its inhabitants? What are its attractions, and how can travelers make preparation for their journey to the country beyond the stars? These and many other questions demand answers. Increasing age and the fact that I shall soon be making my own pilgrimage, have begotten within my soul an intense desire to explore this fascinating subject. Hopefully the following chapters will describe my discoveries.

IVOR POWELL

Heaven Is a Special Place in the Universe

Within the Scriptures the term *heaven* is interpreted in three ways.

(1) The Atmospheric Heaven

This surrounds the planet earth, and from it comes the air we breathe, the rain, clouds, and other elements. Isaiah the prophet had this in mind when he wrote:

> *For as the heavens are higher than the earth, so are my ways higher than your ways, and my thoughts than your thoughts. For as the rain cometh down, and the snow from heaven, and returneth not thither, but watereth the earth, and maketh it bring forth and bud, that it may give seed to the sower, and bread to the eater: So shall my word be that goeth forth out of my mouth . . . (Isa. 55:9–11).*

(2) The Celestial Heavens

This is known as outer space which men are now beginning to penetrate. It is difficult to be definitive regarding distances, but it is interesting to know that scientists are now comparing space and time. They believe both are eternal. They suggest that space also is endless. It goes on and on. This contains the sun, moon, the planets, and innumerable stars. Rockets and man-made machines are now being propelled into the celestial heavens, and the results of explorations are transmitted back to earth.

The ancient Hebrews who ignored the commandments of Jehovah frequently worshiped the stars and sacrificed to "the queen of heaven."

> *Then all the men which knew that their wives had burned*
> *incense unto other gods, and all the women that stood*
> *by, a great multitude, even all the people that dwelt in*
> *the land of Egypt, in Pathros, answered Jeremiah, say-*
> *ing, As for the word that thou hast spoken unto us in the*
> *name of the LORD, we will not hearken unto thee. But*
> *we will certainly do whatsoever thing goeth forth out*
> *of our own mouth, to burn incense unto the queen of*
> *heaven, and to pour our drink offerings unto her, as we*
> *have done, we, and our fathers, our kings and our*
> *princes, in the cities of Judah, and in the streets of*
> *Jerusalem: for then had we plenty of victuals, and were*
> *well, and saw no evil (Jer. 44:15–17).*

The first verse in the Bible states, "In the beginning God created the heaven and the earth." Later in Genesis 1:14 it is stated: "And God said, Let there be lights in the firmament of the heaven to divide the day from the night."

(3) The Sanctified Heaven . . . *the Home of God*
This suggests that heaven is a definite place beyond the stars. When Jesus ascended from the Mount of Olives, "He was taken up; and a cloud received him out of their sight" (Acts 1:9). Paul emphasized that fact in more detail: "[God] raised [Christ] from the dead, and set him at his own right hand in the heavenly places, *FAR ABOVE ALL* principality, and power, and might, and dominion, and every name that is named, not only in this world, but also in that which is to come" (Eph. 1:20–21). The Bible teaches that eventually Christ will return to earth. He will descend from heaven with a shout (1 Thess. 4:16). He will come in the clouds of heaven (Acts 1:11) and will be followed by an immense number of followers riding upon white horses (Rev. 19:14). Many other Scriptures teach that this heaven is the home of the Almighty beyond the stars.

The same truth is evident from the references made to the fall of Lucifer, a created angel who rebelled against the authority of Jehovah and was expelled from heaven. "How art thou fallen from heaven, O Lucifer, son of the morning! How art thou cut down to the ground, which did weaken the nations! For thou hast said in thine heart, I will ascend into heaven, I will exalt my throne above the stars of God. I will sit also upon the mount of the congregation, in the sides of the north: I will ascend above the heights of the clouds; I will be like the most High" (Isa. 14:12–14). Satan was cast out into what might be called a lower heaven. The New Testament describes a second expulsion when "the great red dragon" will be cast out into the earth.

> *And the great dragon was cast out, that old serpent called the Devil, and Satan, which deceiveth the whole world: he was cast out into the earth, and his angels were cast out with him . . . and when the dragon saw that he was cast out unto the earth, he persecuted the woman which brought forth the man child (Rev. 12:9, 13).*

It appears that there was a time when Satan lived in God's country, but was expelled to a lower heaven which became his headquarters. He is called "the prince of the power of the air," and the book of Daniel describes how he interfered with the passage of the angel who was dispatched in answer to the Hebrew's continuing prayers.

> *In those days I Daniel was mourning three full weeks . . . And he [an angel] said unto me, O Daniel, a man greatly beloved . . . Fear not, Daniel: for from the first day that thou didst set thine heart to understand, and to chasten thyself before thy God, THY WORDS WERE HEARD, and I am come for thy words. But the prince of the kingdom of Persia withstood me one and twenty days: but lo, Michael, one of the chief princes, came to help me (Dan. 10:2, 11–13).*

The Bible describes how, in the final days of time, the archenemy of God will be expelled to the earth where he will persecute the Jews and ultimately be condemned for his guilt. To repeat what has already been said, heaven is a definite place somewhere above the earth. It is extremely interesting to know that scientists are now speaking about "a dark hole in space" which until recently remained undiscovered. They say there is something strange about certain parts of the sky, and no one has been able to explain the phenomenon. This may or may not have something to do with the distant heavens, the home of God. It is also true that Jesus ascended—to *somewhere*. If He is to return in the clouds of heaven, He will be returning from where He has been. Somewhere in the universe, God has reserved a place for Himself, and this harmonizes with everything man has been taught.

The earliest native Americans believed their spirits, after death, would go to their happy hunting grounds. Some of the tribes in northern India speak of the land of "*The Shining Ones*." During my years in Africa I was enthralled by the testimony of the pigmy people. When the first missionary spoke about heaven, a native replied, "Oh, we know all about that place. We used to live there." He pointed to a large star and said, "We only came down here to fish in the rivers. But one of our women was greedy. She ate so many fish and became so fat that when she tried to return through that window, she became stuck. Our people could not pull her through from the other side, and we could not pull her back. She remained wedged in that opening, and, unfortunately, we have had to stay here ever since."

Ngobazana's Witch Doctor

During my visit to East London, South Africa, I was invited to speak at the Ministers' Fraternal, and at that meeting I met a little old man, with a neatly-trimmed beard. In company with his ministerial brethren he sat listening, and when I announced that I wished to speak about evangelism, his deepening interest became apparent. There was a strange attraction about that elderly brother, and every few minutes I found myself glancing at him. His restless eyes were looking here and there, and his fingers, with eloquent agitation, tugged continually at his immaculate beard. So I was not surprised when, immediately as the meeting ended, he came across to say, "My brother, I would like to talk with you about your subject. I have been a missionary for over fifty years, and I know a lot about evangelism—native evangelism. When would it be convenient for me to see you?" So a meeting was arranged for the following week.

When he called at the appointed time, he told me of a derelict station where no missionary willingly labored. He spoke of his being sent there, and how he had to cling to God for the necessary grace. He outlined the methods he used in making the once-feared station one of the brightest missionary centers in his part of Africa. It was a grand story, and for someone who had never heard this type of thing the message would have been positively thrilling; but I had heard the same kind of story told by many missionaries, and, remembering the work awaiting me in my room, I wondered how best to terminate the interview. So by way of conclusion I asked him what he considered to be the outstanding event in the whole of his fifty years' missionary activity. He stared hard at me and then looked away into space. He was very still, and for a moment I thought he was about to cry. Slowly he passed his hand across his eyes and then said, "My friend, you ask for my most wonderful experience. I could tell you of many, but of them all the greatest was the conversion of a witch doctor."

Many of my friends have said that I have a "nose" for stories, and I think they are right. When my aged visitor spoke of a witch doctor, I sat right up in my chair and said, "Please tell me about him." As I waited, it was evident that the old minister was living again in the past. A strange glow in his eyes testified to the presence of fires still burning in his heart. I believe he was actually seeing the old village, for he described it so vividly that I saw it too.

There it was, the derelict mission station with its deserted church. Even natives who had once professed conversion had grown indifferent. No one cared for them. Everything and everyone were fast slipping back into heathenism when the faithful servant of God arrived to reclaim some of the lost territory. How he struggled and prayed! Day after day he held on, and at last the desert began to blossom as the rose. The church was cleaned, the services recommenced, and even upon the faces of the Africans new interest was shining. Steadily the work progressed until after many months a flourishing church radiated happiness throughout the entire district. Then came the desire to extend the work. The royal village was many miles away and had no church at all. Would it be possible to obtain permission to build one there? After due prayer and consideration the missionary decided to ask the king. Knowing the chief's daily habit of setting off on some beer-drinking expedition, the missionary arrived early, hoping to find the African in a good mood. He proved to be too early, for when he reached the village the chief was still in bed, and there was nothing to do but wait. Many Africans were waiting also, and, feeling somewhat tired with his journey, the missionary walked a few yards away and sat down on a log. With his head resting in his hands, he was quietly praying about the forthcoming request when suddenly above the noise of the conversations came the sound of someone clearly speaking to the other people. He was saying, "This white teacher is a good man. Yes, he is a very good man and has come to tell us about the great God." The missionary smiled and waited for the usual request for tobacco. The African is a great beggar, and his technique is to preface his request with a preamble of this kind. The missionary waited and the stranger continued, "The white man's God is a very great God—a *very* great God. When we wish to water our gardens, what a lot of trouble we have! We must either dig a long furrow and with patience run the water, or we must keep on carrying it. We get very tired indeed. When the white man's God wishes to water His garden, He sends the rain and it falls on the mountains and the valleys. The forests and all the little plants are watered. What a great God He is! Sometimes I climb to the top of the high mountain, and away over the top of the forest I see the great sea, and God made that also, and yet"—and here he paused— "there is one thing I cannot understand even about the great God. He made the great sea, but wherever did he get so much salt?" Here the missionary laughed outright, for knowing how precious salt is to the natives, he could well understand their wondering at the quantity of salt required for the salting of the ocean! He laughed and sat up, and in a moment the speaker—obviously a witch doctor—was standing in front of him: but not to ask for tobacco.

"Sir, may I talk with you? I have been very ill, and something happened to me. May I sit by your side and talk to you?"

The story that followed filled the missionary's heart with wonder, and although many years had passed when I took the witch doctor's place at the side of the old Christian warrior, that sense of wonder had not departed. As he recalled and retold the story, I also marveled.

"'Sir,' said the African, 'I have been very ill, so ill that my people thought I was dead and began making preparations for my burial. I could see them doing it, and yet I could not move. I knew I would have to show them I was alive, and after a very great effort I managed to move, and they saw me. Yes, I was very ill; but I want to tell you what happened to me. I felt I was in another country. I did not know where, but everything was so wonderful. I was looking at all the beautiful things when a Bright and Shining One came to me, and I was afraid.' He explained that everything was so beautiful because it was God's country. It belonged to the great God who made heaven and earth. He asked me if I knew God, and when I said no, he seemed sad. Then he asked if I would like to see Him, and he took me and showed me."

Here the missionary paused. Then with great deliberation he said, "Mr. Powell, I do not know what you will think of it, but that witch doctor described his vision of God in a way that has lived with me ever since. Even with my education I could not repeat what that ignorant heathen described. In a manner that left no doubt as to his sincerity, he told of this picture of scintillating, shimmering radiance. My brother, I sat enthralled, for not even the evil imaginations of a crafty witch doctor could produce such evident inspiration; but there was more to follow, more that will cause even greater amazement.

"The witch doctor continued, 'I did so want to stay in that wonderful country of God; but the Shining One said, "You cannot stay here, for you do not belong to God. Come with me and I will show you your place." White man, he took me down a long, long passage until at last we came to a big fire. It was like a bush fire. In some places the flames were very big, but in others as if the grass were short, there were only little flames. There were people in all those fires, and I was afraid, for the Shining One said it would be my place, too, as I did not belong to the great God. And then I cried out, "No, no, no! Please let me have a chance. Please let me have a chance." The Shining One looked at me and said, "You shall have a chance. When you wake up, you must find someone who will tell you about the great God. You must be good, and then some day you will be able to come and live in God's country." Then, sir, I opened my eyes and saw the people making ready for my funeral. I did not forget, and, white man, will you tell me how I can know the great God, for I do not want to go to that awful place.'"

Here I interrupted my missionary friend and asked, "Had that witch doctor ever heard the gospel? Had he ever been in contact with Christians? Had he ever seen any Christian literature or the Bible?" My question was anticipated. The old man smiled and said, "I naturally wondered that, too, and made extensive inquiries. The case was so strange that I went to great lengths to ascertain the truth in the matter, and it appeared he had never had any contact at all with anything or anyone Christian. He was a raw heathen and had never heard the gospel. Be it vision, dream, or whatever it was, the message of the country of God was something totally new to him. 'White man,' he said, 'Can you tell me how I can belong to this great God? For some day I shall go back to the Shining One, and I don't want to go into the fire.' There on the log we sat and talked; and seeking a chief's permission to build a church in his village became a thing of secondary importance. I told him the simple story of the gospel, how God sent His Son to save us from hell. Yes, I told him the old-fashioned story of hell, at which so many of my own colleagues scoff. It was difficult to explain, but I tried to enlighten him on the facts of sin and judgment, and how the Lord Jesus came to bear away our sins that we might be forgiven. I told him of heaven and hell, for that was the only way of making him understand the meaning of his vision. When I had finished, I pointed out the various hilltops where some of our people had churches, and said that if he would call there he would hear more of the great God.

"Three months later I received an urgent letter from one of my outstations," the old missionary continued. "It said: 'A witch doctor has been converted.' I guessed who it was, and was not surprised when he arrived at my home one morning asking to be baptized. I tried to explain that first he had to prove his sincerity; he had to demonstrate to all the reality of his conversion. We waited for several months, but every day it became increasingly clear that Ngobazana had lost its witch doctor. He was a new man in Christ, and all the people marveled. Eventually we agreed to baptize him; and what a glorious day it proved to be! He insisted that his baptism should take place in his own village. He wanted to publicly confess Christ in the very place where he had been so wicked. When we arrived, we were amazed to see the crowds that had gathered. People had come from all parts, for the news of what was to happen had filled them with wonder. As we entered the village, the smoke of hundreds of little fires testified to the presence of many people. They were cooking their food for the day.

"We had a great service, and when it ended, the convert invited us to help pull down his old medicine house. The roof, the walls, the bones and charms, and everything else we dragged away to a safe place and made a huge bonfire of them. As the whole lot went up in flames, I could only cry, 'So perish all the works of darkness.' Then came the task of giving a name to our new convert. He said he could not make up his mind which he wanted, David or John. I asked him if he had any objection to having both of them, and at that he was very surprised, for he thought he was allowed only one name. Thus it was decided that the old witch doctor should be called David John, and the name suited him well. All the militant energy and devoted service of the two Bible characters were faithfully reproduced in the convert's life. He refused all work except that of going from kraal to kraal telling of the great vision that had led to his conversion. In every place he would gather his people around him and tell of the great country of God. He would urge upon them the necessity of getting to know the Son of God; for otherwise when they died, they would go into the fire. Thousands of ignorant Africans heard the gospel from his lips, and it might be true to say he was the greatest power for good ever known in that part of the country. His service was so constant and his remuneration so meager that soon his family was in need. Then we made him the official evangelist of our station, and to him this was indeed a very great honor. No word of advice, no effort of mine could restrain his enthusiasm. His people had to be told of the great God and of the fire, and constantly he labored until in a few years he burned himself out. He said he had wasted so many years that it would take him all his time to make up for it."

The story ended, and the Rev. Arthur Edmunds once more sighed and said, "Yes, my brother, that was easily the most outstanding event in my life. I still remember David John's description of the great God, and every time I read of my heavenly Father, the picture supplied by a raw heathen comes before my mind. I wish I could get others to see it, too. I listened to you the other day and said to myself, 'Here is a man after my own heart. He believes in conversion. He has had a vision.' It is so unusual to find a kindred soul, for today the young ministers do not think as we older ones did years ago. You understand me, don't you?" I nodded in agreement. Yes, I understood perhaps far more than he could believe. I shook hands with the old and saintly warrior and walked with him to the gate. He seemed loath to go, and I was sorry he had to leave. His talk had enriched me beyond words, and even now I marvel at David John's vision. How did it happen, since he had never had contact with Christians nor Christian teaching? There can be only one answer—God. Upon that one vision, dream, or whatever it was rested the evangelizing of many thousands of native people. Surely God was responsible for the miracle.

A little later it was my privilege to preach in the Baptist Church at Cambridge, and there I talked with the minister, a son of the celebrated Fred Arnott, the great pioneer missionary. I told him of this wonderful event, and as he listened he gravely smiled and said, "I often heard my father speaking of such dreams. He said that when he first contacted unreached tribes, invariably he found someone who had dreamed such things. Yet, every dream ended with the same feature. Whatever the dreamer had seen or heard, the closing part of his dream was always a command to go to the missionary: He would be able to instruct the dreamer. And when the missionary instruction commenced, the dreams ended."[1]

Notes

1. Condensed from Ivor Powell, *Black Radiance* (London: Marshall, Morgan and Scott, 1949), chapter 6.

There Is a Civilization in the Sky Which Exceeds Anything Known on Earth

The abiding wonders of our eternal home are revealed through various similes within the New Testament.

(1) Heaven Is Called a Country (Luke 19:12)

"*A certain nobleman went into a far country* to receive for himself a kingdom, and to return." Referring to the saints of the Old Testament period, the writer to the Hebrews said: "These all died in faith, not having received the promises, but having seen them afar off, and were persuaded of them, and embraced them, and confessed that they were strangers and pilgrims on the earth. For they that say such things declare plainly that they seek a country" (Heb. 11:13–14). This probably suggests expanse, and its far-reaching greatness.

(2) Heaven Is Called a Kingdom (2 Pet. 1:10–11)

"*If ye do these things, ye shall never fall: For so an entrance shall be ministered unto you abundantly into the everlasting kingdom of our Lord and Savior Jesus Christ.*" This suggests the reign of a monarch, orderliness, authority, and blessedness under the rulership of God. Sir James Jeans in his book *The Universe Around Us* says: "There are more worlds in space above us than there are grains of sands upon all the beaches of earth." God's eternal kingdom could be immeasurably vast!

(3) Heaven Is Called a City (Heb. 11:10; Rev. 21:1–2)

This suggests citizenship and a population which will belong to and reside in the dwellings provided. The fact that Jesus in John 14:2 refers to His Father's house suggests a family, love, and the joy of a continuing fellowship with God.

When the Lord was about to leave this world, He said to His disciples, "Let not your heart be troubled: ye believe in God, believe also in me. In my Father's house *are* many mansions: if it were not so, I would have told you. I go *to prepare a place for you.* And if I go and prepare a place for you, I will come again, and receive you unto myself; that where I am, there ye may be also" (John 14:1–3). It must be remembered that when the Lord spoke about His Father's home, He mentioned mansions or dwelling places *already there*. Then He announced He was leaving to begin a new work to which would be given His continuing attention. "I go to prepare a place for you."

When the Savior uttered those words, the church had not been founded. Therefore, Christians were not to inhabit those "already built" mansions of which Christ spoke. The Lord planned to prepare a special place, and we know now this was to be the New Jerusalem which at the appropriate time would descend from heaven. "And I John saw the holy city, new Jerusalem, coming down from God out of heaven, prepared as a bride adorned for her husband" (Rev. 21:2). "And . . . one of the seven angels . . . talked with me, saying, Come hither, I will shew thee the bride, the Lamb's wife. And he carried me away in the spirit to a great and high mountain, and shewed me that great city, the holy Jerusalem, descending out of heaven from God. Having the glory of God: and her light was like unto a stone most precious, even like a jasper stone, clear as crystal" (Rev. 21:9–11). John described the city as being 1,500 miles square, and at its highest point it reached 1,500 miles into the sky. If it descended upon the United States of America, its western wall would reach from Los Angeles to Vancouver in Canada. The northern wall would go from Vancouver to Toronto, the eastern one from Toronto to Dallas in Texas, and the southern wall from Dallas to Los Angeles. In all probability it would sink, for the earth would not be strong enough to hold the immense structure. Possibly that is the reason why God will need to make a new earth (Rev. 21:1). It has been estimated that the city could accommodate more people than have lived since the days of Adam and Eve.[1]

To repeat what has been said—the mansions mentioned by Jesus were not to be the homes of Christians. Furthermore, they were not to be inhabited by the righteous people of the Old Testament period. These had not yet ascended into heaven. They were awaiting the great parade when the Savior would "lead captivity captive," and escort them into the presence of His Father (Eph. 4:8). When Peter preached on the day of Pentecost he reminded his listeners that "David had not yet ascended into heaven" (Acts 2:34). These facts introduce a very thought provoking question.

For Whom Were Those Many Mansions Erected?

(1) The Bible teaches that somewhere prior to the beginning of time, God created an unknown number of angels to become His servants. The psalmist wrote: "Praise ye the LORD. Praise ye the LORD from the heavens; praise him in the heights. *Praise ye him, all his angels*; praise ye him, all his hosts. Praise ye him, sun and moon praise him, all ye stars of light. Praise him, ye heavens of heavens, and ye waters that be above the heavens. Let them praise the name of the LORD: for he commanded, and they were created" (Ps. 148:1–5). Paul, writing to the Colossians, said: "For by him were all things created, that are in heaven, and that are in earth, visible and invisible, whether they be thrones, or dominions, or principalities, or powers; all things were created by him, and for him" (Col. 1:16).

Throughout the ages of the Old Testament these created beings—the angels—consistently appeared in human form, but they were never seen as animals. Two were named Michael. Jude and John referred to Michael as an archangel (Jude 9 and Rev. 12:7–8). Gabriel appeared to the Virgin Mary (Luke 1:26). The writer to the Hebrews also said: "And again, when he bringeth in the firstbegotten into the world, he saith, And let all the angels of God worship him. And of the angels he saith, Who maketh his angels spirits, and his ministers a flame of fire" (Heb. 1:6–7).

Angels possess bodies which closely resemble human frames. They need places in which to live, for they are not birds, eternally flying in space. Is it possible that when Christ said, "In my Father's house are many mansions," He was speaking about the dwellings of angels?

(2) There are many people who provide a strange, but so far unproven, theory concerning the possibility of intelligent beings in the universe. Their idea seems to be endorsed by inquisitive minds in government. The United States of America has sent into outer space vehicles with special cargoes. Sketches of various types of life to be found on this planet, plus other interesting data, have been included in the hope that if intelligent beings intercept the space craft, they will be supplied with information concerning the human race. In the event of this happening, it is hoped such beings will respond with a similar effort.

The Book of Job supplies thought provoking materials. "Now there was a day when *the sons of God* came to present themselves before the LORD, and Satan came also among them. And the LORD said unto Satan, Whence cometh thou? Then Satan answered the LORD, and said, From going to and fro in the earth, and from walking up and down in it" (Job 1:6–7). Who were the sons of God who came (from somewhere) to present themselves before God?

The proponents of this teaching cite the genealogy found in Luke 3 and especially in verse 38, to substantiate the claim that Adam, the representative head of the human race, was called the son of God. It is also claimed that God created many other intelligent races of beings and that they also had a representative leader. These "heads" were also, by creation, called the sons of God, and that they came from their respective spheres in the empire of God to report to and receive instructions from the Almighty regarding the task of overseeing their part of God's domain.

Certain questions have been asked. (1) What would be thought of a government which built millions of ships and then decided to launch only one? (2) What might be said of an administration which decided to erect millions of homes, and then permitted only one to be inhabited? (3) What could be said of an agricultural commission which plowed billions of fields, and finally decided only one should be planted? Similarly, how could the wisdom and power of God be manifested if He created trillions of worlds and then ordained that only earth should be inhabited? The proponents of this idea believe that intelligent but sinless beings live in other created worlds, that their leaders, like Adam, were called the sons of God, and there was a day when they appeared before the Almighty to receive needed instructions. Adam did not attend, for he had already forfeited any claim he might have formerly possessed—he had sold out to Satan, who attended in his place.

If this be true, there are innumerable dwelling places in God's celestial empire. Nevertheless, it is an established fact that angels exist to serve God and man. "But to which of the angels said he at any time, Sit on my right hand, until I make thine enemies thy footstool? Are they not all ministering spirits, sent forth to minister for them who shall be heirs of salvation?" (Heb. 1:13). Is the interpretation concerning the identity and existence of the sons of God accurate? Candidly, this author does not know.

Notes
1. See Ivor Powell, *What in the World Will Happen Next?* (Grand Rapids: Kregel Publications, 1985), 175–76.

The Citizens of Heaven, Whosoever They Might Be, Are Healthier and More Intelligent Than Humans

(1) The Healthy Angels

"In the end of the sabbath, as it began to dawn toward the first day of the week, came Mary Magdalene and the other Mary to see the sepulchre. And behold, there was a great earthquake: for *the angel of the Lord* descended from heaven, and came and rolled back the stone from the door, and sat upon it" (Matt. 28:1–2). Mark describes the event: "And [the women] said among themselves, Who shall roll us away the stone from the door of the sepulchre? And when they looked, they saw the stone was rolled away: for it was very great. And entering into the sepulchre, they saw *a young man* sitting on the right side, clothed in a long white garment; and they were affrighted" (Mark 16:3–5). Luke wrote: "*Two men* stood by them in shining garments" (Luke 24:4). John supplied another description. "Mary stood without at the sepulchre weeping: and as she wept, she stooped down, and looked into the sepulchre. And seeth *two angels* in white sitting, the one at the head, and the other at the feet, where the body of Jesus had lain" (John 20:11–12).

These accounts become exceedingly interesting when they are compared. Matthew, Mark, and Luke were not present when the women saw the angels; they could only write what they were told. John and Peter arrived later, but did not see the heavenly messengers. There is no discrepancy in the varying accounts. Each detail fits into the complete story.

It is significant that Matthew said, "*the angel of the Lord* descended to roll away the stone. Mark says the women entered into the tomb and saw *an angel* sitting on the right side. Evidently a small party of angels had arrived to share in the greatest event in history. It is thought provoking that the Bible indicates the messengers were angels, but Mark describes them as *young men*.

Probably the angels were created a very long time before Adam and Eve. There is no way by which we can ascertain their exact age; they could have been many thousands of years old, and yet the New Testament describes them as young men. They were ageless—immortal. Among the shining ones from God's world, sickness, hospitals, death, mortuaries, and homes for aged people are unknown. Caskets are never seen in heaven, and headstones for graves are never made. Doctors, nurses, and medical insurance are not required. The planet earth was meant to be a sphere of this type, but, unfortunately, sin ruined God's plans, and the earth became a renegade planet in the universe.

(2) The Intelligent Angels

All distances and speed are irrelevant. "A light year is sometimes used to measure astrological distances. It is equivalent to the distance light travels in a solar year. A light year is equivalent to 5,880,000,000,000 miles" (*Funk and Wagnell's Encyclopedia,* page 5,622). The evolution of speed is a fascinating subject. It was once equal to how fast a man could run or a bird fly. Then with the invention of the wheel came bicycles, automobiles, airplanes, and other machines which revolutionized progress. The space age opened a new world. Rocket propulsion is enabling man to explore the heavens. Vehicles have been launched which, in spite of their enormous speed, will not reach distant planets for many years. The world above us appears to be limitless, and to reach the outer limits of space will take forever! Yet in spite of the apparent difficulties great distances were meaningless to God's angelic servants. They came to earth and departed again without problems.

> *And there were in the same country shepherds abiding in the field, keeping watch over their flock by night. And lo, the angel of the Lord came upon them,*

*and the glory of the Lord shone round about them;
and they were sore afraid. And the angel said unto
them, Fear not: for, behold, I bring you good tidings
of great joy, which shall be to all people. For unto
you is born this day in the city of David a Saviour,
which is Christ the Lord. And this shall be a sign
unto you; ye shall find the babe wrapped in swaddling clothes, lying in a manger. And suddenly there
was with the angel a multitude of the heavenly host
praising God, and saying, Glory to God in the highest, and on earth peace, good will toward men. And
it came to pass, as the angels were gone away from
them into heaven, the shepherds said one to another,
Let us now go even unto Bethlehem, and see this thing
which is come to pass, which the Lord hath made
known unto us (Luke 2:8–15).*

Identical phenomena was witnessed when Jesus ascended into
heaven. "And when [Jesus] had spoken these things, while they
beheld, he was taken up; and a cloud received him out of their
sight. And while they looked steadfastly toward heaven as he went
up, behold, two men stood by them in white apparel" (Acts 1:9–
10).

The disciples watched as the Lord slowly began His journey to
the right hand of the Majesty on High. That, according to facts
already expressed, would be a long way to travel. Yet He made the
return journey in one day. When Mary met the risen Lord, He said
to her, "Touch me not; for I am not yet ascended to my Father: but
go to my brethren, and say unto them, I ascend unto my Father,
and your Father and to my God, and your God" (John 20:17). Evidently, His mission was to ascend to heaven where He would be
crowned with glory and honor (Heb. 2:9). That event was soon
terminated, for, continuing his account, John said: "Then the same
day at evening, being the first day of the week, when the doors
were shut where the disciples were assembled for fear of the Jews,
came Jesus and stood in the midst, and saith unto them, Peace be
unto you" (John 20:19). It must be admitted we have no idea how

this was accomplished. Compared with such knowledge, mankind knows nothing!

Paul declared that Christians will receive bodies "like unto His glorious body." Airplanes will not be needed to travel to a distant destination; the journey will be completed in moments!

There is an interesting story in the Old Testament which tells how an angel smote 185,000 men. It is not revealed how this was done, but it certainly proved God knew how to fight His own battles (see 2 Kings 19:35). There is also another account that contrasts the faith of a prophet with the fear of his servant.

> *And when the servant of the man of God was risen early, and gone forth, behold, an host encompassed the city both with horses and chariots. And his servant said unto him, Alas, my master, how shall we do?. . . And Elisha prayed, and said, LORD, I pray thee, open his eyes, that he may see. And the LORD opened the eyes of the young man; and he saw: and behold, the mountain was full of horses and chariots of fire round about Elisha (2 Kings 6:15–17).*

When Simon Peter drew a sword to defend himself against his enemies, the Lord said: "Put up again thy sword into his place: for all they that take the sword shall perish by the sword. Thinkest thou that I cannot now pray to my Father, and he shall presently give me more than twelve legions of angels?" (Matt. 26:52–53). That was an amazing statement, for Christ claimed to be able to summon at a moment's notice 72,000 angels. Perhaps as some people have suggested, the other world is not so far away as might be imagined.

Scientists declare that if the sun were any closer to the earth, the human race would frizzle; if it were farther away, men would freeze! Supreme intelligence placed it where it is, and that exhibited maximum wisdom. It simply affirms the fact that from every angle heavenly intelligence supersedes anything known upon earth.

Three majestic words express the magnificence of God. They are: omnipotence, omnipresence, and omniscience. God is all powerful, everywhere, and all-wise. By His command worlds came into being. By His power all things exist, and yet, another text inserts into that majestic picture a note of tenderness and compassion.

These are the generations of the heavens and of the earth when they were created, in the day that the LORD God made the earth and the heavens. And every plant of the field before it was in the earth, and every herb of the field before it grew: for the LORD God had not caused it to rain upon the earth, and there was not a man to till the ground. . . And the LORD God formed man of the dust of the ground, and breathed into his nostrils the breath of life; and man became a living soul. And the LORD God planted a garden eastward in Eden; and there he put the man whom he had formed (Gen. 2:4–8).

This is an entrancing picture of God on His knees! Surely He whose word had brought plants into existence could have spoken, and the greatest garden ever seen would have appeared! It is wonderful that the hands that held the universe, should hold a small plant and with great tenderness set it in a special place to please the first human gardeners. Perhaps that was the one and only occasion when the Almighty had soiled hands! Adam and Eve were just two inexperienced people, but God so loved them, He made special provision for their comfort and happiness. It is a logical assumption that the human mind cannot comprehend all that He will prepare to charm those for whom He sacrificed His Son. If we may take a text out of its biblical setting, we can say with Paul, "Eye hath not seen, nor ear heard, neither have entered into the heart of man, the things which God hath prepared for them that love him" (1 Cor. 2:9). Jesus said: "I go to prepare a place for you." There is a world of difference between a garden and the New Jerusalem, but the same hands created both. God could have commanded angels to plant that garden, to arrange its borders, and to set out the flowers that lined its paths. They would have been enthralled to attend to the trees, the shrubs, and every detail of that little bit of heaven upon earth. Yet God reserved that pleasure for Himself. He who inhabited the heavens knelt on the ground and gently placed every plant and flower into its appointed position. It has long since been recognized that mankind could easily live without flowers. They are not essential for human survival. Herbs and other plants with medicinal value were necessary, but flowers revealed that God loves beauty and fragrance. That strange but wonderful statement concerning the thoughtfulness of the Almighty reveals He is not a harsh deity waiting to punish offenders. He is kind, loving, good, and wonderful. All who have met the Savior know this is true, for they have looked into the heart of God.

Angels Are Primarily Our Helpers, Not Our Guardians

The epistle to the Hebrews states: "But to which of the angels said he at any time, Sit on my right hand, until I make thine enemies thy footstool? Are they not all ministering spirits, sent forth to minister for them who shall be heirs of salvation?" (Heb. 1:13–14). It is difficult to avoid the conclusion that this Scripture has been misinterpreted. Angels are not sent to protect Christians. Some teachers sincerely believe God's people are protected from all evil by ministering angels. That was never promised by the writer to the Hebrews. When calamity overwhelms a community, many Christians suffer, lose their homes and other belongings; they sometimes die. It is impossible to believe that through their terrible ordeal they were protected by angels. If they were, the angels went to sleep on their job!

"The authorized version suggests the idea (not conveyed by the Greek Testament) of guardian angels. The more correct translation is: 'Are they not all ministering spirits, for service sent forth, on account of those who are to inherit salvation.' The allusion is generally to their office of subordinate ministration in furthering of the Divine purpose of human salvation. The continuance of such office is indicated by the present participle (apostellomena)."[1]

Many books have been written about the ministry of angels, but few of them mention the dangers connected therewith. Dr. William Barclay says: "There was one danger which the writer to the Hebrews wished at all costs to avoid. The doctrine of the angels is a very lovely thing, but it has one danger. It puts beings between man and God. It introduces a series of beings through whom man approaches God. That is clearly seen in the Jewish belief that angels brought God's message to man, and brought man's prayers to God. In Christianity there is no need for any intermediary person. Because of Jesus and what He did, we have direct access to God. As Lord Tennyson said:

> Speak to him, thou, for He hears
> And spirit with spirit can meet;
> Closer is He than breathing
> And nearer than hands or feet.[2]

Angels are sent by God, not to guarantee safety to endangered Christians, but to offer guidance and give spiritual help to the heirs of salvation. That does not prohibit angels from helping in time of need. Even this author has known at least two occasions when he was saved from death by the gentle push of an unseen hand. Probably the most inspiring illustration of this great truth is supplied by Luke.

> *And he was withdrawn from them about a stone's cast, and kneeled down, and prayed. Saying, Father, if thou be willing, remove this cup from me; nevertheless not my will, but thine, be done. And there appeared an angel unto him from heaven, strengthening him. And being in an agony he prayed more earnestly: and his sweat was as it were great drops of blood falling down to the ground (Luke 22:41–44).*

That ministering angel did not come to earth *to deliver Christ from the tragedy of the forthcoming crucifixion; he came to strengthen the Savior so that He could successfully endure what lay ahead.* Certain preachers have misinterpreted this Scripture. They state that Christ was human, and fearing the approaching sufferings, yearned to escape from His fate. That was not true. Jesus was the Lamb slain from before the foundation of the world.

He came to earth to die for sinners, and according to the writer to the Hebrews, anticipated His death with profound *joy.* "Jesus . . . who for the *joy* that was set before him endured the cross, despising the shame, and is set down at the right hand of the throne of God" (Heb. 12:2). Referring to the Savior, the writer also said: "Who in the days of his flesh, when he had offered up prayers and supplications, with strong crying and tears *unto Him who was able to save him from death—and was heard in that he feared* " (Heb. 5:7). The prayers of the Savior were always answered. When He prayed to be saved from death, *he was saved from death.* That was not the death of the cross, but a premature death in the garden where Satan was endeavoring to kill the Lord. When the blood came from the temples and forehead of Jesus, it became evident that His life was in danger. Had He died in Gethsemane, there would have been no reconciliation, no atonement, no redemption. Christ momentarily feared that might happen and desperately cried to be delivered from a premature death. His prayer was dramatically answered when one of God's ministering angels arrived to impart the necessary strength. Such assistance is available for every Christian. Unfortunately, many are too busy to look for it.

Another text invites investigation. Concerning the temptation of the Lord, Mark says: "And he (Jesus) was there in the wilderness forty days, tempted of Satan; and was with the wild beasts; *and the angels ministered unto him*" (Mark 1:13). There can be no doubt that the extended period of fasting, and the constant harassing from the Evil One, weakened the Lord to such a degree He needed additional strength to offset the efforts of Satan. It is thought provoking that the angels provided what was necessary. Once again let it be emphasized they did not prevent the temptation being made; they provided that which was necessary for the Lord to endure the ordeal successfully.

It is interesting to read Luke's account of Paul's experience in the devastating storm, that wrecked the ship upon which he was traveling to Rome. "And when neither sun nor stars in many days appeared, and no small tempest lay on us, all hope that we should be saved was then taken away. But after long abstinence Paul stood forth in the midst of them, and said, Sirs, ye should have hearkened unto me, and not have loosed from Crete, and to have gained this harm and loss. And now I exhort you to be of good cheer: for there shall be no loss of any man's life among you, but of the ship. *For there stood by me this night the angel of God*, whose I am, and whom I serve, Saying, Fear not, Paul; thou must be brought before Caesar: and, lo, God hath given thee all them that sail with thee" (Acts 27:20–24). Evidently, that ship could not sink before the appointed time. The angel of God did not prevent Paul and his companions from getting wet, but he did bring them to the shore. Wise people never grumble in the storms of life; they look for God's angels.

These Scriptures suggest a very challenging question. Since the angels know what is happening upon the earth, are they with us all the time, or are they specially commissioned by the Almighty to help in time of need? Apart from the miraculous speed with which angels travel, it seems difficult to believe they belong to a home far away.

Billy Graham, the famous evangelist, has written a best-selling book about angels, in which he says: "As an evangelist I have often felt too weary to minister to men and women who filled a stadium to hear a message from the Lord. Yet, again and again my weakness has vanished and my strength has been renewed. I have been filled with God's power, not only in my soul, but physically. On many occasions God has become specially real, and has sent His unseen, angelic visitors to touch my body, and let me be His messenger from heaven speaking as a dying man to dying men and women."

Dr. Paul Lee Tan tells a remarkable story concerning something which happened in the life of Queen Victoria of England. He writes, "The British express railway train raced through the night, its powerful headlamp spearing the darkness ahead. The train was carrying Queen Victoria. Suddenly, the engineer saw a startling sight. Revealed in the beam of the train's headlight was a weird figure in a black cloak, standing in the middle of the tracks and waving its arms. The engineer grabbed for the brakes and brought the train to a grinding halt. He and his companions climbed down to see what had stopped them, but they could find no trace of the strange figure. On a hunch, the engineer walked a few yards up the track. Suddenly, horrified, he stared into the fog. The bridge had been washed out, and had toppled into the swollen river. If he had not heeded the ghostly figure, the train would have plunged into an abyss. While the bridge and the tracks were being repaired, the train's crew made a more intensive search for the strange flagman, but the mystery was not solved until they returned to London.

At the base of the engine's headlamps, the engineer discovered a huge dead moth. He looked at it for a moment, and then on impulse, wet its wings and pasted it to the glass of the lamp. Climbing back into his cab, he switched on the lamp and saw the "flagman" in its beam. Then he realized what had taken place. The moth had flown into the beam seconds before the train was due to reach the washed out bridge. In the fog it appeared to be a phantom figure waving its arms. When Queen Victoria was told of the strange happening, she said: "I'm sure it was not an accident; it was God's way of protecting me."[3]

Mark states that after the Resurrection, the Lord "appeared *in another form* unto two of them, as they walked, and went into the country" (Mark 16:12). Christ *came in disguise!* There is reason to believe He still does. Happy are the people who can recognize Him whenever He comes, and in whatever form.

Notes

1. "Hebrews," in *The Pulpit Commentary*, ed. Joseph Exell (Grand Rapids: William B. Eerdmans Publishing Co., 1950), 21:17.
2. Quoted from William Barclay, "Hebrews," in *Daily Study Bible* (Philadelphia: Westminister Press, 1976).
3. Paul Lee Tan, *Encyclopedia of 7,700 Illustrations* (Rockville, MD: Assurance Publishers, 1988), 129–30.

There Was a Day When "The Saints Went Marching In"

When he ascended up on high, he led captivity captive, and gave gifts unto men (Eph. 4:8).

Mention has already been made that the Old Testament saints did not go immediately to heaven when they died. Sin had only been covered by the blood of sacrifices, but this enabled God to continue His association with guilty people. The Savior plainly taught this truth when He delivered the parable of the rich man and Lazarus. He described how the beggar died and was carried by the angels into Abraham's bosom; the rich man died and went to Hades. Christ also indicated that there was recognition in the place of the departed, for Abraham asked that Lazarus be permitted to bring water to quench his thirst. *Hades*, which is the equivalent of the Old Testament *sheol*, was divided into two sections. The unrighteous dead were separated from the righteous by an impassable gulf (see Luke 16:20–31).

When the Lord died, He put away sin by the sacrifice of Himself and removed the hindrance which had denied entrance into the presence of His Father. That made possible the glorious entry of the saints into the hallowed precincts of God's home. One of the first things Christ did after His death was to visit the one section of hades to announce that deliverance was at hand. According to the teaching of Paul, when Jesus went home to be our High Priest, He led a multitude of captives who had become His delighted followers. Their arrival in God's country must have been one of the most joyful celebrations ever witnessed by angels.

It was never revealed in what order the believers went, but everyone from Adam until the day of Christ's ascension was in that glittering procession. Perhaps Adam and Eve were the first to follow the Savior, and thereafter Abel and Seth, Isaac and Rebekah, Jacob and his family, Moses and the elders of Israel, Elijah and Elisha, Samuel and all the prophets proudly followed. People who had been "stoned, they were sawn asunder, were tempted, were slain with the sword, they wandered about in sheepskins and goatskins; being destitute, afflicted, tormented, (Of whom the world was not worthy). They wandered in deserts, and in mountains, and in dens and caves of the earth. And these all, having obtained a good report through faith, received not the promise: God having provided some better thing for us, that they without us should not be made perfect" (Heb. 11:37–40). That glorious parade of believers provided the most glittering spectacle ever witnessed in God's country. Their arrival in heaven must have been something for which preparation had already been made.

(1) Where Did They Reside?

It has been ascertained that Christ had already testified to the many mansions existing in His Father's home. Perhaps these were built by angels and erected in readiness for the moment when millions of God's people would come marching triumphantly into the glory land. Each time I traveled into a foreign country, reservations were made in hotels, etc., and when I arrived, I was escorted to my appointed place. Did such a thing happen when the saints arrived in their new homes? Did angels explain many things to the new arrivals?

(2) Did These People Have Glorified Bodies?

When Moses and Elijah appeared on the Mount of Transfiguration to speak with Jesus about His death, both had bodies. Does that suggest that all the Old Testament believers had received bodies that would never age? They resembled the glorified body of the Redeemer. It would seem rather unnecessary for angels to build mansions for people who were spirits.

(3) Did They Require Food—If So, What Did They Eat?

It would be marvelous if authentic answers to these and many other questions could be provided. When the disciples found it difficult to believe their Lord had risen from the grave, He did certain things to strengthen their faith. Luke says: "And while they yet believed not for joy, and wondered, he said unto them, Have ye here any meat? And they gave him a piece of a broiled fish, and of an honeycomb. And he took it, and did eat before them" (Luke 24:41–43). It is therefore safe to assume His body had digestive organs and everything else necessary for receiving food. We do not know how spirits exist, but bodies need food.

(4) Did They Have Shops and Merchandise for Sale?

There will be cities, towns, and villages throughout God's empire, with innumerable homes or dwelling places. There will be miraculous transportation, etc., but there are other things of which we have little or no information. If food is to be eaten, will it be grown? Will it be sold in shops? If so, what kind of currency will be used? It is known that heaven will be a place of music, for John described how a magnificent choir will sing the song of Moses and the Lamb. We know there will be ten thousand times ten thousand, and thousands of thousands who will be thrilled to fill God's country with music. Will there be a mammoth choir practice, and convened festivals in specially constructed auditoriums? When royal balls are arranged in London, England, the Queen makes a special appearance, and is welcomed by an appreciative audience. When such occasions are arranged in heaven, will *the King of Kings* leave His palace and proceed along streets of gold to be acclaimed by His devoted subjects? Will the continuing interest in music give birth to the making of harps and other instruments? When John described how the Lamb opened the book with seven seals, he said:

> *And he came and took the book out of the right hand of him that sat upon the throne. And when he had taken the book, the four living creatures (beasts), and four and twenty elders fell down before the Lamb, having*

> *every one of them* harps, *and golden vials full of odours,*
> *which are the prayers of saints. And they sung a new*
> *song (Rev. 5:7–9).*

(5) Will There Be a Clothing Industry?

When angels were mentioned in the Scriptures, they were clothed with long white garments. When John described the return of the Savior, he wrote: "And the armies which were in heaven followed him upon white horses, *clothed in fine linen*, white and clean" (Rev. 19:14). Does that statement mean the noble steeds will be housed in special stables with their own attendants? If there be sightseeing trips for visitors from distant places, will the royal stables be on the lists of attractions?

(6) Will the Saints in God's Country Know Each Other?

The Rev. Charles Haddon Spurgeon, the famous British preacher, was asked this question by an anxious woman. His reply was made instantly. "Woman, do you think we shall be greater fools up there than we are down here?" That answer is not a satisfactory one for people who desire evidence from the Scriptures. Describing what happened on the Mount of Transfiguration, Matthew wrote:

> *And after six days Jesus taketh Peter, James, and John*
> *his brother and bringeth them up into a high mountain*
> *apart, And was transfigured before them: and his face*
> *did shine as the sun, and his raiment was white as the*
> *light. And, behold, there appeared unto them Moses and*
> *Elias talking with him. Then answered Peter, and said*
> *unto Jesus, Lord, it is good for us to be here: if thou wilt,*
> *let us make here three tabernacles; one for thee, and one*
> *for Moses, and one for Elias (Matt. 17:1–4).*

It would be most informative if we knew how Peter recognized the heavenly visitors. He had never seen them, for they belonged to a bygone age. As far as it is known, photography was an unknown science in those days, and New Testament records do not say that Jesus introduced His friends from a bygone age. Yet Peter recognized the two messengers. Is it too much to assume that since he knew them, so shall we? If we shall know people we never met, we shall surely know those whom we have seen and loved during our sojourn on earth.

When I became a Christian, I lost all my friends and became almost a recluse as, night after night, I read my Bible. At that time I did not possess any other books. My imagination was very active and I read of the mighty exploits of God's indomitable servants. In thought I went with David to meet Goliath and listened to Elijah as he addressed the crowd on Mount Carmel. I stood alongside Simon Peter when he preached on the day of Pentecost. I remember those early experiences in my Christian life and feel assured that if I am able to visit my boyhood heroes in the next world, I shall ask many questions which my friends will be delighted to answer. Years ago during an open air gospel service a colleague said something about Jonah who was swallowed by the great fish. A man interrupted, challenging what had been said. My friend responded: "Well, I will wait until I get to heaven and will ask him." "And what if he is not there?" The preacher responded: "Then you can ask him."

(7) Will There Be Children in Heaven?

No one can doubt the fact that the Savior loved boys and girls, and His words: "Suffer the little children to come unto me, for of such is the kingdom of heaven" remains one of the most loved of all His statements. When Zechariah described the future of Jerusalem, he wrote:

> *Thus saith the* LORD*; I am returned unto Zion, and will dwell in the midst of Jerusalem: and Jerusalem shall be called a city of truth and the mountain of the* LORD *of Hosts the holy mountain. . . . And the streets of the city shall be full of boys and girls playing in streets thereof (Zech. 8:3, 5).*

That Scripture has been partially fulfilled on many occasions; its ultimate fulfillment will take place when Jerusalem becomes the capital city of Christ's earthly kingdom. It would be wrong to say this text refers to heaven. We know that angels were described as young men, suggesting that age as we know it will be abolished. Could the same thing be true of very young children—will they be seen as *young people*? That is, if a baby dies on earth, will that child be seen as he would have been had he not died in infancy? When people questioned the Lord concerning a possible difficulty in heaven, He replied: "Ye do err, not knowing the Scriptures, nor the power of God. For in the resurrection they neither marry, nor are given in marriage, but are as the angels of God in heaven" (Matt. 22:29–30). Marriage was blessed by God so that births could replace what was lost through death. There will be no need for replacements in heaven; there will be no death.

Let it be admitted we are trying to understand things which challenge the human intellect. Nevertheless, the effort is justified, for the redeemed of the Lord will not be expected to sit throughout eternity content to do nothing!

When Christians Die, They Go Immediately into God's Presence

Therefore we are always confident, knowing that, whilst we are at home in the body, we are absent from the Lord. (For we walk by faith, not by sight:) We are confident, I say, and willing rather to be absent from the body, and to be present with the Lord. Wherefore we labour, that, whether present or absent, we may be accepted of him (2 Cor. 5:6–9).

It is regrettable that many church people do not agree with the teaching of Paul. They retain the idea that Christians, when they die, go to some intermediary place where they are purified and prepared to enter into the presence of God. Throughout the ages misguided clerics made a great amount of money exploiting this idea, claiming their prayers could shorten the period of time souls stayed in purgatory. *Funk and Wagnell's Standard Reference Encyclopedia* states:

> Purgatory is a place of pergation in which, according to the Roman Catholic Church, and Oriental churches, souls after death are purified from venial sins, and undergo a tempered punishment which, after the guilt of mortal sin has been remitted, still remains to be endured by the sinner . . . The Medieaval doctrine and practice of Purgatory were among the grounds of the protest of the Waldenses, and were rejected by the Reformers. Protestants replied to the arguments of the Roman

Catholics on the subject of purgatory, by refusing to
admit the authority of the Church Fathers. A belief in
an intermediary state, and a period of education and
probation on the other side of the grave, is widely taught
by the Anglican Church.

The Reformers rejected this doctrine because it was not sup-
ported by the New Testament.

Paul believed that when the soul left the body it proceeded immediately into the presence of the Almighty. He taught that every
sin which prevented that access was removed by the precious blood
of the Redeemer. Christ opened a new and living way into the
presence of God. Whatever obstacle existed prior to His death was
removed when Christ made reconciliation for sin and never reap-
peared. When the apostle described the death of a Christian, he
said the departing soul was *absent* from the body, and *at home*
with the Lord. If a person is absent from any place, he cannot be
present.

A very argumentative woman came to me at the close of an
evangelistic service to say I was a deceiver of the Last Day. She
believed in "soul sleep." That is, so she explained, when a Christian dies, he remains in his casket until the day of resurrection.
She was annoyed when I said, "Lady, I do not like caskets that
much!" Forcefully, she responded, "Whether you like them or not,
that is where you will be." I told her she was misinformed, but
when I quoted Paul she became angry and said, "Bah! Who was
Paul? He was just another misguided man."

If redeemed souls remain in their decaying bodies or stay asleep
in caskets, something was ineffective in the atoning work of the
Savior, and the sacrifice of Christ did not remove every obstacle
between the righteousness of God and the need of mankind.

When the dying thief sought and obtained forgiveness, Christ
said, "Today shalt thou be with me in paradise." He did not say,
"Go to sleep and someday I will awaken you." The Lord intended
to take the thief with Him—wherever He was going. It was significant that when the first Christian martyr, Stephen, was about
to lay down his life, he said: "Behold, I see the heavens opened,

and the Son of man *standing* on the right hand of God . . . and they stoned Stephen, calling upon God, and saying, Lord Jesus, receive my spirit. And he kneeled down, and cried with a loud voice, Lord, lay not this sin to their charge. And when he had said this, he fell asleep" (Acts 7:56–60). This great text contrasts with something said in the epistle to the Hebrews. "But this man, after he had offered one sacrifice for sins for ever, *sat down* on the right hand of God" (Heb. 10:12). It is believed the Lord rose from His throne of splendor to welcome home the first Christian martyr. Although it is recorded that devout men carried the body to its burial, Stephen was already on his way to meet the Lord. The dying thief and Stephen were the firstfruits of a great harvest of precious souls.

Concerning the return of the Savior, Paul wrote:

> *For the Lord himself shall descend from heaven with a shout with the voice of the archangel, and with the trump of God: and the dead in Christ shall rise first: Then we which are alive and remain shall be caught up together with them in the clouds, to meet the Lord in the air: and so shall we ever be with the Lord (1 Thess. 4:16–17).*

Young Christians sometimes find difficulty in understanding this message. They ask: "How can the dead in Christ be raised if they are already in His presence?" This is not a problem when the fact is considered that the body is the earthly home of the believer. It is unfortunate that even the most wonderful bodies die. The tenant—the soul—vacates the earthly tabernacle and proceeds into the presence of the Lord. It is not known whether the homegoing Christians will be given a temporary body, or will, for a while, remain as a spirit in God's world. It is written that "God is a Spirit, and they who worship Him must worship Him in spirit and in truth." It is known, however, that they who believe in Christ will inherit bodies like Christ's glorious body. Paul wrote:

> *For our conversation (citizenship) is in heaven; from whence also we look for the Saviour, the Lord Jesus Christ: who shall change our vile body, that it may be*

fashioned like unto his glorious body, according to the working whereby he is able even to subdue all things unto himself (Phil. 3:20–21).

The transformation of the human body will take place when Christ returns for His bride, the church. The Bible teaches that the Savior will bring His saints with Him, the trumpet will sound, and the dead (bodies) in Christ will rise first. Then those which are alive and remain will be caught up together with them to meet the Lord in the air. It is also written that the church will reign with Christ on earth. Bodies will be essential when saints occupy important positions in the kingdom of Christ. His servants will not be sunbeams floating around the streets of Jerusalem. Paul was very explicit when he explained:

Behold, I shew you a mystery; We shall not all sleep, but we shall all be changed. In a moment, in the twinkling of an eye, at the last trump: for the trumpet shall sound, and the dead shall be raised incorruptible, and we shall be changed. For this corruptible must put on incorruption, and this mortal must put on immortality. So when this corruptible shall have put on incorruption, and this mortal shall have put on immortality, then shall be brought to pass the saying that is written, Death is swallowed up in victory. O death, where is thy sting? O grave, where is thy victory? (1 Cor. 15:51–55).

The Christian who returns with his Lord will receive that new body and be ready to accept any assignment given by the King of Kings. The Bible does not support the doctrine of "soul sleep." That type of thing ended when Jesus opened the gates of hades and took His people home. Matthew described another event that happened at the resurrection of the Savior.

Jesus, when he had cried again with a loud voice, yielded up the ghost. And behold, the veil of the temple was rent in twain from the top to the bottom; and the earth did

> *quake, and the rocks rent; And the graves were opened, and many bodies of the saints which slept arose, And came out of the graves after his resurrection, and went into the holy city, and appeared unto many (Matt. 27:50–53).*

Having completed their mission, those saints then overtook other ascending believers and they went home together.

Since that amazing time the Holy Spirit has been active upon earth, helping, instructing, and purifying the church which one day will be presented as a bride without blemish to the Lord. Paul said: "Christ also loved the church, and gave himself for it; That he might sanctify and cleanse it with the washing of water by the word, That he might present it to himself a glorious church, not having spot, or wrinkle, or any such thing; but that it should be holy and without blemish" (Eph. 5:25–27). Meanwhile, when a Christian dies, his or her spirit goes immediately into the presence of God. What takes place at the moment of arrival in heaven is a matter of conjecture.

Many years ago when I ministered in Glasgow, Scotland, an elderly woman on her way home slipped on the wet ground and fell into the River Clyde. A young man who was passing by went immediately to her rescue and succeeded in bringing her to the bank. Not desiring publicity for his act, he hurried into a side street and was never identified. The medical men who were summoned to the scene assisted the old lady, and eventually she opened her eyes. As she began to remember her fall, she realized someone had rescued her and, looking at the attendants, said, "I want to see the one who saved me!" Probably that kind of request has been heard millions of times in heaven. When I shall open my eyes in my Father's country, I shall be filled with amazement as I see the surroundings. Then I shall realize where I am. I believe I will say, "I want to see the One who saved me!" He will be there, hopefully, to lead me to the palace of His Father. Maybe He will say, "Holy Father, he is home at last." If God shall answer and say, "Well done, thou good and faithful servant, enter thou into the joy of thy Lord," my heaven will be two heavens in Immanuel's land.

What would I desire next? I think I would want to meet my

loved ones who preceded me to heaven, and who have waited a long time for my arrival. If they do not know already, I shall have much to tell them about things that happened after they left Wales. Sometimes I believe I have more friends in heaven than upon earth, for as I become older, increasing numbers of associates have gone to live in the land of endless day. Perhaps my family will take me to see things which God has prepared for those who love Him. I am persuaded that as the lights of heaven grow brighter, those on earth will become increasingly dim. F. White and Robert Harkness must have been inspired when they wrote the words and music of my favorite hymn:

> I have heard of a land on a far away strand,
> In the Bible, the story is told
> Where cares never come; never darkness nor gloom,
> And nothing shall ever grow old.

> There are evergreen trees that bend low in the breeze,
> And their fruitage is brighter than gold.
> There are harps for our hands in that fairest of lands,
> And nothing shall ever grow old.

> There's a Savior who died, and His arms are spread wide,
> Pardoned sinners like me to enfold.
> And I know when I stand in that beautiful land,
> His glory will never grow old.

> There's a home in that land, at the Father's right hand
> There are mansions whose joys are untold.
> And perennial spring where the birds ever sing,
> And nothing shall ever grow old.

> In that beautiful land on that far away strand,
> No storms with their blasts ever frown.
> The streets I am told, are paved with pure gold,
> And the sun it shall never go down.

Christ Is the Heavenly Representative of His Church

Seeing then that we have a great high priest, that is passed into the heavens, Jesus the Son of God, let us hold fast our profession (Heb. 4:14).

We are about to consider what happens in the high court of heaven, but to prepare for the study, it is necessary to remember remarkable discoveries that have revolutionized life on earth. I remember when as a child I was envious of a neighbor who had made a crystal wireless set. He was proud of his achievement and patiently explained to our family how his contraption worked. I had seen a magician pulling a rabbit out of a tall hat, but it mystified me how our friend pulled music out of thin air!

Years later in London I sat in a crowded apartment to see my first television program. It was not very good, for the picture was covered with white "snowflakes" which appeared out of control. We were fascinated, for the transmission showed members of the royal family. The host apologized for the poor reception but explained we were forty-six miles from the studio, and that was the range of the broadcast. He predicted things would improve, and his promise has been fulfilled. I remember when my father, who never saw television, would wait a week for a broadcast of a special football game. At the appropriate moment he would switch on his "wireless set," and would be asleep within one minute! When he awoke, he asked who won the game. Today astronauts journey into space and relay information back to earth.

The progress made is beyond description, but it should always be remembered man did not invent either radio or television. They were secret possibilities discovered in the universe. If Abraham had possessed the know-how, he could have listened to radio and watched television. These things have become so commonplace that even small children take them in their stride. A few years ago, at Christmas, my wife was sweeping our driveway when two loud booms echoed from the sky. A small boy of about five years was riding his new tricycle down the street, and she said to him: "Did you hear that? Maybe that was Santa Claus returning to his home at the North Pole." The lad grimaced and with all the wisdom of a five-year-old replied: "That wasn't Santa Claus—that was a sonic boom."

If mankind has been able to discover so many amazing things in the universe, the question may be asked: "How many other secrets still await discovery?" Recently I saw my first telephone-television picture. The operator apologized for the poor reception but explained the science was still in its infancy. I also saw a man flying onto a football field, and I wondered if someday every individual will be able to emulate his example and travel like birds. This leads to a startling fact. God, who made the universe, knows every possibility in it, and therefore, in trying to visualize what happens in His world, we must consider things which here belong only to fantasy.

We have computers in which the personal history of every citizen of earth may be safely stored, and recalled at the touch of a button. Since Christ is the representative or High Priest of millions of His followers, and angels are secretaries who keep records, do they use machines beyond our comprehension? The Bible mentions "writing" in the Book of Life. For example, Jesus said, "Notwithstanding in this rejoice not, that the spirits are subject unto you; but rather rejoice, because *your names are written in heaven*" (Luke 10:20). It was necessary to use that terminology, for had He spoken of computers, His disciples would have been mystified. It is now possible to take a closer look at something that happens daily in God's country.

The writer to the Hebrews wrote almost exclusively about the high priestly work of the Savior, and in proof thereof, based his thesis on the description, sacrifices, and effectiveness of the ancient tabernacle. He was not referring to theories or fanciful ideas, but to things that actually existed and happened. Since heaven is a place with cities, streets, mansions, and other things, it is a reasonable assumption that God's country includes an area where Christ's ministry is performed.

Heaven's Hall of Justice

This truth has been implied all through the Bible. When sin ruined the earliest form of human civilization, God said: "My Spirit shall not always *strive* with man" (Gen. 6:3). "There are two Bible words, which, pregnant with meaning, offer the most suggestive word-pictures. Dr. Strong declares that the Hebrew word *doon* (translated strive) really means 'to struggle; to resist a charge of murder.' Liddle and Scott maintain that the Greek word *agonizomai* which is also translated '*to strive,*' means the same thing. Therefore, to appreciate the full significance of these Scriptures one must endeavor to see a law court where a desperate lawyer anxiously examines records, sifts each piece of evidence, and does everything possible to gain a verdict on behalf of the accused."[1]

When the Hebrews became a nation, their leader, Moses, was told to erect a tabernacle so that Jehovah could live among His people. Explicit instructions were given concerning its size, services, and sacrifices. The most vital of all the commands related to the Holy of Holies where God's presence would be found at the mercy seat. It was significant this was not called the judgment seat. The High Priest on the Day of Atonement was permitted to enter into the presence of God to intercede on behalf of his people. He wore a breastplate upon which were the names of the tribes. Although apparently no words were spoken, the inscription above his heart indicated he was the representative of unworthy sinners who depended upon the mercy of God. He placed one spot of blood upon the altar and seven spots before it. If the nation had neglected or rejected God's commandment, they would have perished. Many sacrifices were offered daily, but what happened on the Day of Atonement was reserved for one special day of each year. Thus did God teach His people the importance of the offering and the priest. Attached to the hem of the sacerdotal robe were small bells, and whenever the priest moved, the music of the bells was clearly heard. Then the listeners rejoiced, for they knew their representative was alive—the sacrifice had been accepted, and they were safe. The law said that without the shedding of blood there was no remission (Lev. 17:6).

The High Priest was Israel's only intercessor; he was the one mediator between God and man. He continued in office until the end of his life when he was succeeded by another appointee. The same ritual was followed when Solomon built the temple. God made sure that every person in Israel became aware of the importance of the offering and of the man who placed the blood upon the altar.

When the writer to the Hebrews wrote his letter, he explained what had transpired throughout the ages had been a foreshadowing of that which was to come.

> *For Christ is not entered into the holy places made with hands, which are the figures of the true; but into heaven itself, now to appear in the presence of God for us; Nor yet that he should offer himself often, as the high priest entereth into the holy place every year with blood of others; For then must he often have suffered since the foundation of the world: but now once in the end of the world hath he appeared to put away sin by the sacrifice of himself (Heb. 9:24–26).*

Somewhere in the city of God is a place where this ministry is exercised—an elegant hall of justice where records are preserved, ministering angels work, and the Lord Jesus Christ, our High Priest, intercedes for every believer. He is our attorney—or lawyer—or advocate—in the court of heaven. The apostle John, when giving advice to his friends, said:

> *My little children, these things write I unto you, that ye sin not. And if any man sin, we have an advocate with the Father, Jesus Christ the righteous (1 John 2:1).*

If we confess our sins, he is faithful and just to forgive us our sins, and to cleanse us from all unrighteousness (1 John 1:9).

I made my purchases in a supermarket and was approaching the cashier when a lady who was speaking with the owner of the store looked at me, and said: "Oh, I know you. You are an attorney." I smiled and replied, "No, lady, I am not an attorney, but I know a great one. He has never lost a case, and has never charged for his services." She responded: "Go on! Honest! You know a lawyer who never lost a case and never charges a fee? Go on! What's his name?" I replied: "Lady, His name is Jesus." For a few seconds I thought she was having a heart attack. She swallowed hard, and her face became very red. But my attention went to the store owner who was very excited. His arms had been raised above his head; he was jumping up and down and yelling: "That's right, Mister. Jesus! He never lost a case and never charges a penny for what He does. That's right, Mister. That's right." Evidently he was a Christian.

Occasionally I try to visualize the hall of justice in God's celestial city, and imagine my name being mentioned by an old enemy. It is thought provoking that Satan is called "The accuser of the brethren." John said of him: "And I heard a loud voice saying in heaven, Now is come salvation, and strength, and the kingdom of our God, and the power of His Christ: for the accuser of our brethren is cast down which accused them before our God day and night" (Rev. 12:10). Some day the Devil will be unable to continue his evil work, but for the present time, for reasons we cannot understand, he is permitted to enter into the presence of God to make insinuations concerning the guilt and unworthiness of God's people. As a prosecuting counsel he demands that I should be found guilty on every charge brought against me—those accusations could be many. It is extremely difficult to agree with Paul when he claimed to be the "chief of sinners" (see 1 Tim. 1:15).

Yet when the accusations ceased, even Satan would be surprised when the counsel for the defense, my great High Priest, quietly, convincingly, said: "He has been forgiven. I took his place, received his condemnation, paid his debt, and set him free." "Verily, verily, I say unto you, He that heareth my word, and believeth on him that sent me, hath everlasting life, *and shall not come into condemnation*; but is passed from death unto life" (John 5:24). Then the Judge of heaven would gently say: "Ivor Powell is accepted in the beloved. The case is dismissed." I do not think God would clear His court of applauding angels. Praise is commonplace in God's country. The Savior said: "I say unto you, that likewise joy shall be in heaven over one sinner that repenteth, more than over ninety and nine just persons, which need no repentance" (Luke 15:7). Such a scene would be impossible if the angels were spirits without bodies, drifting as clouds in the sky. I believe every facet of God's country will be extremely beautiful. Every gorgeous and wonderful exhibit of the creative art will be reproduced in a superb fashion. God did not create lovely things like the song of a lark, the fragrance of flowers, a deer peacefully grazing on a forest path, only to outlaw them in His own intimate world. There will be many wonderful sights in God's country, but none will surpass in excellence the wounds in the Savior's hands, the evidence of the price He paid for our admittance.

Notes
1. Ivor Powell, *Bible Highways* (Grand Rapids: Kregel Publications, 1959), 9.

Our High Priest in Heaven Is Unique—One of a Kind

For we have not an high priest which cannot be touched with the feeling of our infirmities; but was in all points tempted like as we are, yet without sin. Let us therefore come boldly unto the throne of grace, that we may obtain mercy, and find grace to help in time of need (Heb. 4:15–16).

For there is one God, and one mediator between God and men, the man Christ Jesus; Who gave himself a ransom for all, to be testified in due time (1 Tim. 2:5–6).

The text is interesting, for the word translated *touched* is *sumpatheesai*, from which is derived the English verb *to sympathize*. The writer desired to emphasize that unlike members of the Aaronic priesthood, Christ understood all the problems confronting His followers. He had traveled the same pathway, carried similar burdens, and been confronted by overwhelming difficulties. The Lord came to earth to share our laughter and tears. Every trusting believer can say with Job: "But he knoweth the way that *I* take: when he hath tried me, I shall come forth as gold" (Job 23:10). Our High Priest was, is, and ever will be unique—He remains one of a kind! There will never be another like Him.

Many years ago when I was a young man, I became associated with a band of itinerant evangelists known in Britain as "The Pilgrim Preachers." The leader, Mr. Ernest Luff of Frinton on Sea in Essex, was beloved by multitudes of people. His long white beard gave him the appearance of a patriarch, and his wise counsel attracted many people. I considered him to be the most Christlike person I ever met. I shall always remember visiting a town where the local leaders shared a very difficult situation. A lady in the church had suffered a nervous breakdown after the death of her husband. No counselor could help; her faith had been eclipsed. When Mr. Luff was asked to visit her, he gladly consented to do so.

I was with the other members of our party when he returned. His face reflected the sorrow in his heart when he said, "Boys, I failed in my mission. She was kind and hospitable. She listened patiently to all I said, but then she asked a very simple question. 'Sir, have you lost your wife? If not, you cannot know how I feel. You still have your partner, but I am alone. Thank you for trying to help me, but you have not walked my path of life and, therefore, cannot understand how I feel.'" When my friend placed his head into upturned hands, I thought he was about to weep. The writer to the Hebrews believed no Christian could ever use such words when speaking of the Savior. Christ knows everything about us, and *He cares.*

> Lord, help me never to forget
> That Thou art now my Friend;
> That every detail of my life
> Thou plannest to the end.
> Sometimes when troubles round me lie,
> When clouds obscure my sky,
> Help me O Lord, to know and feel
> That Thou art always nigh.

The epistle to the Hebrews was written to people who were in danger of losing their faith. The customs observed for many generations had been destroyed; the temple was in ruins, apparently God had ceased to care for His people. The writer reminded his readers that God had provided far better things than had been lost. The word *better* is the key word of the epistle, and is found throughout the chapters. The author mentions: Better Things (6:9), A Better Hope (7:19), A Better Testament (7:22), A Better Covenant

(8:6), A Better Promise (8:6), A Better Sacrifice (9:23), A Better Substance (10:34), a Better Country (11:16), A Better Resurrection (11:35), and A Better Provision (11:40). These texts are reminders of a better country, a better resurrection that takes us there, and the better sacrifice that made entry into God's kingdom possible. The letter emphasizes that the Lord Jesus Christ is infinitely better than any priest who preceded Him. He is unique and beyond comparison! There are at least eleven reasons for this assertion.

Reason 1. He shed His own blood.

"But Christ being come a high priest of good things to come, by a greater and more perfect tabernacle, not made with hands, that is to say, not of this building; Neither by the blood of goats and calves, *but by His own blood* he entered in once into the holy place, having obtained eternal redemption for us" (Heb. 9:11–12). Every priest from Aaron to the time of Christ offered sacrifices, but no one offered his own blood, for it was tainted. Priests were sinners needing forgiveness for personal transgressions. Christ, who was tempted by Satan, remained without sin, and that was the reason His sacrifice was acceptable to God.

Reason 2. His one sacrifice was sufficient.

"But this man, after he had offered *one sacrifice* for sins for ever, sat down on the right hand of God" (Heb. 10:12). It has been estimated that at each Passover, millions of lambs were provided to meet the demands of worshipers. It would be impossible to assess the number of sacrifices offered since the days when Moses instructed Israel to follow this procedure. Turtledoves were brought by poor people, lambs by the middle classes, and oxen by wealthy land-owners. Throughout Jewish history, billions of sacrifices had been brought to the priests. Christ offered Himself *once*, and that was sufficient.

Reason 3. He went where no other priest was permitted.

"For Christ is not entered into the holy places made with hands, which are the figures of the true; but *into heaven itself*, now to appear in the presence of God for us" (Heb. 9:24). Every Jew realized the danger of displeasing Jehovah. When God came down to speak with Moses on Mount Sinai, the tribes were warned not to approach the mountain. They were told that if they disobeyed, they would die. Even priests were not permitted to enter the Holy of Holies. The High Priest was allowed to enter once a year, but that was the limit of his opportunities. It was impossible for any man to rise into the sky and enter God's country. Yet, the Savior did that for us. It is a stimulating thought that Christ looked into the face of His Father, and at the same time He had our names upon His lips.

Reason 4. The effects of His ministry were eternal.

The priests who ministered during the Old Testament dispensation were required to offer many sacrifices every day. The people of Israel returned again and again because of their continuous need. The Bible says: "Neither by the blood of goats and calves, but by his own blood he entered in once into the holy place, having obtained *eternal redemption* for us" (Heb. 9:12). The assurance of salvation rests upon this fact. Through time and eternity Christ will meet the need of those who trust Him. The poet was correct when he wrote:

> My name from the palms of His hands
> Eternity cannot erase;
> More happy—*but not more secure*,
> The glorified spirits in heaven.

Reason 5. Christ's ministry is unlimited.

The high priest of Israel represented the entire nation, and yet, unfortunately, his personal attention was not given to everybody. Lepers were outcasts and had no opportunity of meeting a priest unless they had reason to believe they had been cleansed. Even the ministers in the temple were human and could become infected by unclean people. The Savior was remarkably different from all others. He touched unclean lepers and gave them assistance which no other could supply. This ability was not only seen in His contact with diseases; He also helped outcasts of society. The woman whom He met at Sychar's well had to draw water at midday, when other citizens were not in the vicinity. Christ made a special journey to meet this despised soul and then used her testimony to reach a community (John 4:40–42).

Reason 6. Christ was more than human.

"Seeing then that we have a great high priest that is passed into the heavens, *Jesus, the Son of God*, let us hold fast our profession" (Heb. 4:14). When my wife and I first went to South Africa, there were 93,000 would-be immigrants on the waiting list ahead of us. The Baptist churches in that country urgently needed my services, and it was extremely fortunate that a very important official within the government belonged to one of our churches. His influence performed what appeared to be a miracle. We arrived in time for the first scheduled meeting. It never hurts to have a friend in high circles! That truth applies to the government of heaven. When insurmountable problems confront us, our High Priest intercedes, and the impossible becomes possible.

Reason 7. Christ is a royal high priest.

"Thou art a priest for ever after the order of Melchisedec" (Heb. 7:17). The ancient priest who appeared to Abraham remains one of the most mysterious men mentioned in the Bible. His was the most important of all the appearances known as *theophanies— appearances of God in human form*. Apart from the Savior, this man was the king of Salem, and a priest of the Most High God (see Heb. 7:1). He might have been considered a mystical person from antiquity, but the Bible also says He was "Without father, without mother, without descent, having neither beginning of days, nor end of life, but made like unto the Son of God; abideth a priest continually" (Heb. 7:3). As a priest, Christ interceded; as a king, He will rule. He can do what others cannot.

Reason 8. This High Priest sat down at God's right hand.

"God . . . Hath in these last days spoken unto us by his Son, whom he hath appointed heir of all things, by whom also he made the worlds; Who being the brightness of his glory, and the express image of his person, and upholding all things by the word of his power, when he had by himself purged our sins, *sat down on the right hand of the Majesty on high*" (Heb. 1:2–3). "Now of the things which we have spoken this is the sum: We have such an high priest, *who is set on the right hand of the throne of the Majesty in the heavens*" (Heb. 8:1). "But this man, after he had offered one sacrifice for sins for ever, *sat down on the right hand of God*" (Heb. 10:12). When a potentate in eastern countries desired to show favor to any person, he was invited to occupy a seat at the king's right hand. Evidently God was pleased with everything Christ did, and that included the intercession for His followers.

Reason 9. This High Priest has a greater following than any other.

"Wherefore he is able also to save them to the uttermost *that come unto God by him*, seeing he ever liveth to make intercession for them" (Heb. 7:25). It appeared inconceivable that from a cross on a hill outside of Jerusalem Christ's love should charm millions of people. Israel's high priest only ministered to those who belonged to the twelve tribes. Occasionally, but not often, a few proselytes came from Gentile nations, but beyond that, God's people included only Hebrews. Other people were considered to be aliens. It is thrilling to read the testimony of the singers in heaven. "And they sung a new song, saying, Thou art worthy to take the book, and to open the seals thereof; for thou wast slain, and hast redeemed us to God by thy blood *out of every kindred, and tongue, and people, and nation*" (Rev. 5:9).

Reason 10. The music of this High Priest fills eternity.

Mention has already been made of the small bells attached to the hem of the robe worn by the high priest of Israel. When he moved, listeners heard the music and rejoiced, knowing their sacrifice had been accepted. Perhaps this relates in some measure to the singing of the immense choir in God's country. John wrote: "And I beheld, and I heard the voice of many angels round about the throne and the beasts (living creatures) and the elders: and the number of them was ten thousand times ten thousand, and thousands of thousands; Saying with a loud voice, Worthy is the Lamb that was slain to receive power, and riches, and wisdom, and strength, and honour, and glory, and blessing" (Rev. 5:11–12). Calvary will never be forgotten—not even in eternity. Christ will always be the Lamb that was slain—He will be known by the print of the nails in His hands.

Reason 11. Christ was the only priest who promised to return to earth.

"So Christ was once offered to bear the sins of many; and unto them that look for him shall he appear the second time without sin unto salvation" (Heb. 9:28). When an Old Testament priest died, his body was buried and his work continued by a man appointed to succeed the deceased. No official ever promised to return to earth to continue his labor. Christ will fulfill the type given through Melchisedec. At the present time He is our High Priest, interceding before the throne of God. Some day He will be the Royal Priest, for He will reign in Jerusalem for one thousand years. "And in that day there shall be a root of Jesse, which shall stand for an ensign of the people; to it shall the Gentiles seek: and his rest shall be glorious" (Isa. 11:10). "They shall not hurt nor destroy in all my holy mountain; for the earth shall be full of the knowledge of the Lord, as the waters cover the sea" (Isa. 11:9).

Perhaps All the Citizens of Heaven Will Be Bilingual

Speech is a means of communication. It can be expressed by the spoken word, the written word, or by signs. Without these methods of expression understanding would be severely handicapped. Probably, because Christians in many nations have the Scriptures in their own language, they have assumed too much. When I asked a friend what language would be spoken in heaven, she replied instantly, "Why! English of course!" Actually, she had never thought about this matter and assumed that when she went to heaven there would be no need to change her form of speech. A similar answer would be given by people of all nations. An Indian, a European, a Chinese, a Japanese, and all who are readers of the Bible in their own language would readily assume their form of speech will be used throughout God's country. The history of languages used in the Bible is worthy of consideration.

Unlike the rest of mankind, Adam and Eve were never children attending a school. They appeared on the scene when they were young adults and apparently never studied the grammar of any language. Yet Adam was able to supply names for every animal, tree, and plant which God had created.

> And out of the ground the LORD God formed every beast
> of the field, and every fowl of the air; and brought them
> unto Adam to see what he would call them: and what-
> soever Adam called every living creature, that was the
> name thereof (Gen. 2:19).

That was a remarkable achievement. I knew a family with many children, and I smiled when the parents confessed that finding names for all of them was a difficult task. When I read that God brought every form of life to Adam *that he might supply names for them all*, I felt sorry for my earliest ancestor. Adam was not a dummy! He named the elephant, the hippopotamus, the horse, and every kind of dog and cat. Apart from new species which resulted from crossbreeding, Adam gave names to everything on the earth. It would be interesting to know what language he used. Today all mankind has different names for these forms of life, for the Scriptures have been translated into many tongues. It would be fascinating if we knew the actual names given by Adam to the forms of life created by God. Was the language identical with that spoken by Jehovah when He said, "Let there be light" (Gen. 1:3)? Was it the same used by the divine family before time began?

The first man and his wife never learned how to speak, and we are compelled to believe language was given to them and with it, an amazing understanding. If the same thing had happened to me, I would have had fewer headaches learning how to speak English! Many years passed, and ultimately an ancient writer was able to report: "And the whole earth was of one language, and of one speech" (Gen. 11:1). I remember one of my archaeological friends in Australia explained how ancient artifacts had provided evidence that proved the catastrophe concerning the Tower of Babel had really happened. He said that clay tablets had been discovered upon which was a sketch of a fish and three scratches. These indicated what the customer wished to purchase and how many. When language was not understood, the purchaser devised means to make known his desires. The Bible describes how Jehovah thwarted the schemes of ancient builders by confounding their language. The people were unable to understand each others' speech. Thereafter men and women were scattered in all directions, and the diversity of languages began. Who spoke what was never revealed. Was the method of speech formerly used by God continued, and did this become the official language of the Hebrew nation? If so, there might be some justification for the theory that Hebrew was, and might be, the language of God's heavenly empire. The additional forms of speech which spread throughout the world gave birth to innumerable dialects that caused innumerable headaches for missionaries.

When Jesus was a small child, He was undoubtedly taught to speak the language used by the Jewish nation. At a later date when the Feast of Pentecost was being celebrated in Jerusalem, God did something that was unprecedented. The gospel message urgently needed to be sent around the world. Thousands of people who were attending the feast were planning to return to their distant homes, and the possibility existed that each could be a preacher of good tidings, but the men could not explain things beyond their comprehension.

> *And when the day of Pentecost was fully come, they were all with one accord in one place. . . . And they were all filled with the Holy Ghost, and began to speak with other tongues, as the Spirit gave them utterance. And there were dwelling at Jerusalem Jews, devout men,* out of every nation under heaven . . . *And they were all amazed and marvelled, saying one to another, Behold, are not all these which speak Galileans? And how hear we every man in our own tongue, wherein we were born? Parthians, and Medes, and Elamites, and the dwellers in Mesopotamia, and in Judaea, and Cappadocia, in Pontus, and Asia, Phrygia, and Pamphylia, in Egypt, and in the parts of Libya about Cyrene, and strangers of Rome, Jews, and proselytes, Cretes and Arabians, we do hear them speak in our tongues the wonderful works of God (Acts 2:1–11).*

This was one of the greatest miracles ever performed. Later within the newly formed churches, the practice of speaking in a strange tongue was widely practiced, but it was always necessary that an interpreter be present to explain what was being said. The apostle Paul, in trying to prevent confusion said: "If any man speak in an unknown tongue, let it be by two, or at the most by three, and that by course; and let one interpret. *But if there be no interpreter, let him keep silence in the church*, and let him speak to himself, and to God" (1 Cor. 14:27–28). It is fascinating to remember there were not any interpreters in the streets of Jerusalem when the Holy Spirit enabled vast crowds to understand what Peter was saying in his remarkable sermon. I have always considered that the miracle of Pentecost was that everybody was able to understand in his own tongue what was being preached. There is no biblical support for the assumption that meetings were being held on many street corners and that foreigners were running all over the city trying to find someone speaking their particular language. It would be difficult to believe that an Ethiopian was trying to find a meeting where he could understand what the speaker was saying. Listeners had no need to learn a new language, and the Pentecostal preachers were not expected to study intensely to be able to deliver their message. When visitors returned to their homes they repeated what they had heard, and the spread of the gospel was assured. Thus did the Lord prepare the way for the missionary journeys of Paul, and before the end of the apostle's life the gospel was heard throughout the known world. What happened on the Day of Pentecost was never repeated.

That introduces a very important question. Was this strange tongue identical with the language spoken in heaven? Will this become the vehicle of communication between the redeemed from many nations? On the other hand, it would be strange if, when I arrive in God's country, I shall be required to abandon my native tongue. I have spoken to the Lord in English for over eighty years, and I am sure He understood what I was saying. I have parents, friends, and many converts awaiting my arrival in heaven. We spoke together on earth in a language we understood. When I meet them in God's country, I hope to begin again where I finished here.

Some people might say this reasoning is conjecture. They could be correct. Nevertheless, this explains why the suggestion has been made that all citizens in God's country may be bilingual. Maybe when we meet old friends we shall converse in our native tongue. When we meet others in God's family, we might speak in a language known throughout the length and breadth of God's empire. This entire subject is filled with speculation, and it would be unwise to become dogmatic about things of which God has not spoken. If the apostle Paul were here he could—if he so desired—enlighten us about many things. When he wrote to the Corinthians, he said: "It is not expedient for me doubtless to glory. I will come to visions and revelations of the Lord. I knew a man in Christ above fourteen years ago (whether in the body, I cannot tell; or whether out of the body, I cannot tell: God knoweth;) such an one caught up to the third heaven. And I knew such a man (whether in the body, or out of the body, I cannot tell: God knoweth;) How that he was caught up into paradise, and heard unspeakable words, which it is not lawful for a man to utter. Of such an one will I glory, yet of myself I will not glory; but in mine infirmities" (2 Cor. 12:1–4).

Paul proceeded to explain why the Lord permitted "a thorn in the flesh" to trouble him; it was God's messenger helping to sustain the apostle's humility. Curiosity would like to ask Paul several questions: 1) What did he see in paradise? 2) Why was it illegal to describe what he saw? 3) What language was used in Paul's experience? 4) Was Paul glad to be back on earth, or would he have preferred to remain where he was?

Henry Richards was one of the oldest members in the church where I became a Christian. He was approaching ninety years of age, and could neither read nor write. However when he prayed, maybe all the angels listened and laughed. He had heard someone explaining how Paul had been caught up into paradise, but had been forbidden to describe his experiences. Henry thought about this, and as usual, reported back to God in the prayer meeting. He said: "O, God. I thank You that we have not been told what heaven is like. If we knew, we would all be committing suicide to get there fast. We might get there too soon, and You would have to send us back to earth." That old Christian was not a theologian, but sometimes his prayers expressed true wisdom.

Heaven's Administration Has Strict Immigration Laws

The United States of America has many immigration problems; for citizens of other nations consider this to be the most attractive place in the world. Unfortunately it is very difficult to gain admittance into this land. Shiploads of illegal immigrants pay enormous sums of money to be transported close to our shores, and some even try to enter via Mexico. These desperate people are observed by the Coast Guard authorities, apprehended, and sent back to their native land. Every night Mexicans cross the border, and the patrols are unable to catch them all. The search for these unwanted aliens continues in San Diego and Los Angeles, where they are often found working in the sweat shops of the great cities. These people live in constant dread of being caught and deported. The situation is alarming, and many observers believe the problem will never be solved.

I learned many years ago that there is a right and a wrong way of trying to enter the United States. My wife and I had been the official guests of the Baptist churches in South Africa, New Zealand, Australia, and Canada, but when we were invited to work in California, we became apprehensive. We had heard that some people had been refused admittance. We read numerous books and interviewed many folk. Our greatest help came from those who had already become citizens of the United States. They explained how certain procedures had to be followed; visas obtained, etc. We listened attentively to all that was said and never argued with anybody. We wanted to be sure everything would be satisfactory to the authorities.

The day will never be forgotten when, anxiously, we approached the official at the border. He looked us over and then asked for our documents. If I had been foolish, I might have said, "Sir, I do not need any documents. I am 'The Man from Wales' and am known all around the world." He would have been very surprised, but I am convinced he would have replied, "I don't care if you are the Man from Mars. Your documents, please." I was not stupid; I gave my papers to him. He read and stamped them, and said, "Sir, welcome to our country."

When I reminisce, I recall the intense desire with which I tried to please everybody associated with my entering America. Since that day I have traveled extensively in other lands, and I have always been impressed by the efficiency of the officials at our ports of entry. They possess huge books in which are printed the names and addresses of every citizen of the United States. The official looked at our passports, consulted his records, and asked: "Do you still live at 612 Surf View Drive, Santa Barbara, California?" "Yes, sir, I do." "Good. Welcome home. I trust you had a wonderful vacation." That always reminds me of my Father's country, where a similar procedure is followed. Heaven's administration has a tremendous book called "The Lamb's Book of Life," and in it is inscribed the name of every person who claims citizenship in heaven. If my name were not in the American book, entry would be denied. The Bible says that if any name is not found written in God's book, entrance into *His* country is impossible (see Rev. 20:15).

It is therefore a matter of paramount importance that one's name be inscribed in God's records. Some men face approaching death and wonder what lies beyond. They wistfully say, "If only someone had returned from heaven to supply information concerning what is needed." Alas, death is terminal. No human has ever returned to earth to tell us anything. Foreseeing that necessity, God arranged a special way of acquiring knowledge. Through the medium of a vision John was transported to heaven to see and hear things which otherwise would have remained unknown.

> *And one of the elders answered, saying unto me, What are these which are arrayed in white robes? and whence*

> *came they? And I said unto him, Sir, thou knowest. And*
> *he said to me, These are they which came out of great*
> *tribulation, and have washed their robes, and made*
> *them white in the blood of the Lamb. Therefore are they*
> *before the throne of God, and serve him day and night*
> *in his temple (Rev. 7:13–15).*

I am reminded again of the time when I was preparing to enter the United States of America, and how I interviewed people who had accomplished what I hoped to do. Their advice was invaluable. John wrote about people who were *already in heaven* and then supplied information about how their entry was made possible: "*They washed their robes and made them white in the blood of the Lamb.*" The text suggests three important details.

(1) Here Is Cleansing Supplied by God

God alone can supply cleansing for the human soul. He provided the sacrifice to obtain the skins to make the first garments for humans (Gen. 3:21) and the ram which became a substitute for Isaac when death seemed imminent and inescapable (Gen. 22:13). Jehovah also sent the Lamb of God who took away the sins of the world (John 1:29). The Savior spoke of a king who planned a reception for his son and arranged that a special wedding garment be provided for each guest. Unfortunately, a man rejected the garment and was instantly noticed by the king and expelled from the company (see Matt. 22:1–14). At infinite cost, God provided the garments of salvation for all invited to the marriage of His Son, but guests are expected to accept what is offered and be grateful.

(2) Here Is Cleansing Accepted by Man

"*They* washed their robes and made them white in the blood of the Lamb." That statement implies certain things: (a) *Their Recognition.* People do not wash garments which are clean! Ladies do not purchase expensive dresses and immediately send them to the dry cleaners. Women launder clothes because they realize the garments are soiled. The fact that these citizens of heaven had washed their robes indicated they had concluded their robes were unfit to be worn at a royal banquet. (b) *Their Responsibility*. God provides the cleansing and the Holy Spirit enlightens the soul regarding its need. Nevertheless, the sinner himself must decide what course of action will be followed. A woman may stand for hours looking at soiled clothing, but unless she starts her washing machine, her laundry will never be cleaned. God does many things for His people, but He never destroys man's ability to choose. A person may fervently believe a city bus can take him to a destination. He may have complete confidence in the driver's ability to operate the vehicle, but unless he occupies a seat, he will be left standing in the street. (c) *Their Response*. "They washed their robes." They did not postpone the act—*they did it*. When they availed themselves of what God had provided, their robes became as white as snow. The poet asked important questions when he wrote:

> Have you been to Jesus for the cleansing power?
> Are you washed in the blood of the Lamb?
> Are your garments spotless,
> Are they white as snow,
> Are you washed in the blood of the Lamb?

(3) Here Is Cleansing Recognized by Heaven

John explained that these people were not hoping to enter heaven—*they were already there*. Whatever demands were made by the immigration officials of heaven, these people had been accepted and welcomed. They were established citizens of God's country and were serving Him day and night in His temple. They were not admitted because of their honorable lives, giving to the poor, supporting their church, or because they had been model citizens in a community. These characteristics were not considered of value when someone sought admittance into the kingdom of God. Many of the saints would have qualified had those attributes been acceptable; but even they knew human merit was not the factor that made citizenship possible. Therefore, forgetting all earthly qualifications, those redeemed souls accepted what the Lord provided and thus avoided any difficulties which might have arisen at heaven's port of entry.

I know a place where sins are washed away,
I know a place where night is turned to day;
Burdens are lifted,
Blind eyes made to see;
There's a wonder-working power
In the blood of Calvary.

I have a great friend, a minister who planned a trip to Israel and was enthralled by the prospect of visiting the Holy Land once again. He packed his bags, said good-bye to his family and friends in Florida, and proceeded to New York to board his flight to Tel Aviv. Unfortunately he forgot to take his passport, and at the last moment the trip had to be canceled.

John Bunyan, who wrote "The Pilgrim's Progress," mentioned a character who suffered a similar fate. He climbed over a wall to enter the Christian Highway. He should have entered by the normal road which led to a Green Hill, but he considered that to be unnecessary. He walked with Christian all the way to the Celestial City only to discover he had no passport! He was so near to the Kingdom of God and yet so far away.

Young Christians may have difficulty understanding the terminology of the Bible. The New Testament leaders wrote about being washed in the precious blood of Christ, and some immature believers may consider this to be gruesome! Let it be understood that people are never immersed in the blood of anybody. The Bible urges its readers to "rightly divide the word of truth." Moses taught that life was in the blood (see Lev. 17:11). When God's servants spoke of the blood of Christ, they were thinking of His sinless life; when they spoke of His *shed* blood, they were referring to His life outpoured at the Cross. The members of the early church knew they had been accepted by God—not because of any merit of their own, but through faith in the Redeemer. According to New Testament writers, the precious blood of Christ makes peace with God (Col. 1:20), brings sinners to God (Eph. 2:13), cleanses the soul (1 John 1:7), opens a highway into the presence of God (Heb. 10:19), purges the conscience (Heb. 9:14), and provides victory for embattled saints (Rev. 12:11). Everything enjoyed by Christians was won through the redeeming work of the Savior.

When a soul repents of sin and surrenders to Christ, all that was accomplished at Calvary becomes effective on his behalf. Corporations spend enormous sums of money to install electricity over vast areas. They organize sources of supply, place lines over thousands of miles, and install apparatus in millions of homes. Finally, the pushing of a simple switch brings radiance. Similarly, God went to great lengths to establish His network of Good News. Yet, in the final analysis, it is faith which "pushes the switch." Without it, men remain in the dark; with it, they are able to say, "Once I was blind, but now I can see. The light of the world is Jesus."

There Are No Custom Houses in Heaven

Be not thou afraid when one is made rich, when the glory of his house is increased; for when he dieth he shall carry nothing away (Ps. 49:16–17).

Travelers who arrive in heaven never bring luggage! Hence, they have nothing to declare; a Bureau of Customs is unnecessary; anything of value must be sent ahead. That was exactly what the Lord recommended to His disciples when He said:

Lay not up for yourselves treasures upon earth, where moth and dust doth corrupt, and where thieves break through and steal. But lay up for yourselves treasures in heaven, where neither moth nor rust doth corrupt, and where thieves do not break through nor steal: For where your treasure is, there will your heart be also (Matt. 6:19–21).

Many years ago when I was the minister of a church in Wales, a man came to my home seeking help. He desired to make his last will and testament, but because he had no experience in this kind of thing, he wondered if I could assist. He smiled when I asked if he were contemplating death, and replied, "No, Minister, but you never can tell." He waited while I filled in the introductory details of the official document and, when I was ready, proceeded to describe how he wished his estate to be administered. He began by informing me what he desired to leave for his widow. Then he outlined what he wished his son and daughter to inherit. Finally, he leaned back in his chair and said, "That's it."

I wanted to be quite sure I had not made any mistakes, so slowly I read back to him all that had been written. When I had finished, he said, "Good. They will all have something." He was bewildered when I casually asked, "How much will you have?" He stared at me, and replied, "Parson, don't be silly. I'll be dead." I answered, "Of course you'll be dead, but when a man travels overseas he makes provision that he will not arrive penniless. He either transfers cash or carries traveler's checks. Now you cannot take anything with you when you go to God's country, but it is possible to arrange that you will not arrive a pauper. You have carefully arranged that each member of your family will inherit something, but what will you possess in the next world?" His reply was instantaneous and startling. "Good God, I never thought about that!"

Opening Graves with a Fountain Pen

I stared at him and wondered if he were being silly. He was just an ordinary kind of fellow, and not one I should naturally connect with any hair-raising, blood-curdling adventures, and yet he had just informed me about his opening a tomb. He had disinterred the buried!

As a boy I reveled in stories of nocturnal escapades. In fancy I often rode with outlaws and sailed with pirates, but cemeteries and graves were horrid. I shuddered each time I saw them, and yet here was a man who had enjoyed opening a grave; he had sought and found a corpse; he had brought it back into the world. I could only stare at him.

His old eyes twinkled merrily. He was enjoying his joke, as, with renewed emphasis, he repeated his claim. He had just come from the graveyard. When he explained that it was the Bank of Scotland, I really did think his mind was unbalanced! I did not betray my thoughts and casually asked him to explain. His eyes suddenly became serious as he looked into my face and said, "My brother, most people put their money in the bank, and *never see it again*. It's buried. Oh, yes they may draw a little now and then, and, of course, it's always there should it ever be required. All that is true, but most people never see their cash again. At the end of the year they receive an account. They eagerly scan the balance sheet, but fail to realize that the bank's figures are but memories of the dead! Yes," he repeated, "I know they could draw one, two, or more thousands; but how many do? They have sufficient for ordinary needs, so the rest lies buried for ever. They die, and relatives quarrel over the tomb and its contents. Folk dream of lost treasure. The world went crazy with excitement when archaeologists unearthed the gold of an ancient king. But what happened to the recovered gems? They were immediately buried again, only this time in a glass coffin in the National Museum of Egypt! And if the average man found another enormous treasure, what would he do with it? Maybe he would spend a bit and enjoy a bigger and better house, etc., but when the novelty of spending had passed, he would take the residue and bury it forever in the bank—the national cemetery—and never see it again.

"Well, my brother, I have just been down to my grave; I have shifted some of the debris and looked at my buried friend. My! I'm just beginning to get a kick out of life. You find it hard to understand me, don't you? You want to know how it all came about. I can answer that, too. I was walking through a wood one morning, when everything in nature seemed to be praising God. The lovely trees, so tall and stately; the hills, so silent yet so eloquent; the birds with their sweet music; everything was just grand. I spoke with the Savior: 'Lord Jesus, I have so much money in my pocket, and I have so much in the bank. Would You like some of it? If You want some for any special purpose, Lord, You are very welcome to it.'

"And, my brother, it was at that moment I discovered the location of the National Cemetery! Many of God's servants are hindered through lack of financial support whilst fortunes lie buried. Missionary enterprise is seriously curtailed because Christians sing, 'Take my silver and my gold,' and do not mean what they sing. Do you wonder why I opened my grave? Are you surprised that I dug up my golden corpse? I asked the Lord what I had to do, and He told me, and, brother, I'm really living now."

᠔ᴀ ᠔ᴀ ᠔ᴀ

In the north of India a gray, dusty road runs through the hills into Tibet. It's a strange road in a strange country, and if we could be there to watch it, we should see many strange sights as daily the mysterious and dusky sons of the East pass along it. Beyond lies Tibet, so precious to Christ, and yet so out of reach, for His lovely name is rarely heard in that closed land of temples. Missionaries would sacrifice a great deal for the privilege of taking the light to those who sit there in darkness, but the years come and go, and Tibet is still closed. Her peoples come out, and they eventually return by that winding, dusty, hilly road.

A few years ago a missionary sat looking down at that highway, and as he sat, he dreamed of a rest-house. It would be just the thing. Through its portals would go the weary travelers, and as they rested and listened, they would ask, "But who is this Jesus who died for us?" And the story of the Savior's love would be told again. A little later, renewed in strength, they would continue their journey, but possessing something new. They had heard of His fair name, and secreted within the mysterious folds of their garments would be some tracts, telling yet more of the Christ of the Cross.

Oh, it would be wonderful! But the dream faded. The light went from the seer's eyes. The road was still there; the people, weary and ignorant, were still there, and where the road-house had stood in his dream was just an open space—waiting, calling, challenging.

That missionary had a very sympathetic hearing when he appealed to his society for a financial grant. "I must have my road-house," he cried. But the kindly directors could only listen in silence—there was no money. "But I *must* have it," he said again. They knelt down and prayed, and God told a man to open a grave!

That road-house is now there, beside the distant highway. The dream has come true. Some of my friend's resurrected treasure made it possible. He cannot preach, he plays no outstanding part in any society or meeting, but in one thing he is expert—he's an excellent grave digger!

❧   ❧   ❧

In the heart of an African forest is a clearing where stands a pretty little hospital, an island of peace in a turbulent, dark ocean of trouble. There missionaries fight against overwhelming odds. Doctors struggle to attend to everyone's needs, but the list of sufferers daily grows longer, causing lines of worry on the faces of the staff. If only they all had ten lives to give for Christ and Africa!

Not so very far away is a leper colony. Leprosy—that scourge of countless thousands, the dread of whole continents. Brave men and women indeed are these great-hearted Christian doctors. Daily they come to grips with this pestilential tyrant, and often they win the battle. No tongue or pen can adequately describe the scenes. These men and women work from dawn till bedtime, with no other reason than that "the love of Christ constrains" them. And yet they only touch the fringe of the need. Oh, for more help! And India, and China, and Africa, and the islands of the sea take up the cry, "Oh, for more help!"

At a desk in a British university college sits a bright-eyed student. Her father is a proud man, blessed with mixed fortunes—a brilliant girl and an empty pocket. He watches that girl as she successfully passes the preparatory examinations, yet he secretly grieves, for soon it all must end. Then my friend commences grave digging! The girl is now a medical student and someday may devote her abundant capabilities to Africa, China, or India. Resurrected gold from that grave pays all her fees.

"Aye, brother," said my friend, "you think reopening graves is a mucky job. No! No! It is the greatest occupation in the world."

❧ ❧ ❧

Another friend of mine, a missionary, rather shocked me with his stories of field difficulties. Sometimes expenses run high, and private finances are completely exhausted. The aim is always to make the station self-supporting, but that is not easily accomplished. A pioneer missionary has often to "live off the land," which can be hardship indeed. Not all frames take kindly to some types of native food, and when home assistance fails at a crucial moment, grievous indeed may be the trial.

The realization of this, in my opinion, must make the task of a missionary society's treasurer the most worrisome of all jobs. Such posts demand men of a mighty faith who can shoulder burdens unbearable to others. There was a morning in a certain missionary office when an honored servant of the society was reading his large correspondence. In a very insignificant envelope was a check for £1,000. One can imagine how the face of the recipient lit up. One thousand pounds for the mission field! What a blessing! Salaries could be paid, other needs supplied, and the general work on the field advanced in all sorts of wonderful ways. Had that faithful servant of God been told that the gift had come from "the tomb," he might have wondered if the donor were a simpleton and the check invalid. It was not the only check, for a similar amount was sent out from that same source. Yes, my friend reveled in his new job. In fact, he excelled at opening graves with a fountain pen!

№ № №

Now for a contrast. In a certain English city years ago a very keen Christian introduced to his committee a project heavy upon his heart. When he might have been resting, hours of the night had been spent planning, praying, hoping. Now everything was complete. The committee's sanction would set the whole machinery working, and ultimately thousands of souls would hear the blessed gospel. He propounded with enthusiasm his theories and explained his plan. £1,000 was required—a mere trifle, surely, when so much depended upon it.

The committee listened in complete silence. He was an irresistible man—but £1,000! A member coughed and slowly rose to his feet. "Gentlemen, the thought is good, very good; the plan undoubtedly sounds as though it may be workable, but where in all the world does our esteemed brother expect to find his £1,000? It cannot be done. And, Gentlemen, even if our honorable friend advances the money himself, who will be responsible for maintenance afterward? £1,000. Good gracious! It's preposterous!"

He sat down. Within two months that man died and left £89,000. His mortal remains followed his money—to the grave. "Where in all the world does our esteemed brother expect to find his £1,000?" How easily he himself might have supplied the answer! He could have financed the whole scheme and would never have missed the money. Had he done so, what a welcome would have been waiting for him in the sky!

I seem to hear my friend again. His words ring in my ears. "Brother, it's a great job; and, mind, it is easy when you know how to do it. Do you remember how Joseph of Arimathaea opened his tomb for Christ? We must do likewise." Then he paused awhile; he appeared to be thinking deeply. I wondered what he would say next. I had not long to wait. "Yes, we must do likewise, but it cannot be done unless we possess three things. Would you like to know those three essentials? I'll tell you—A big heart! A steady hand! A spot of ink!"[1]

If my friend ever owns a pen in God's Country, I believe it will be made of gold and studded with diamonds. That man surely knew how to lay up treasure in heaven.

Notes
1. Ivor Powell, *We Saw It Happen* (London: Marshall, Morgan and Scott, 1948).

At the Present Time Heaven Must Be Filled with Intense Activity

For we must all appear before the judgment seat of Christ; that every one may receive the things done in his body, according to that he hath done, whether it be good or bad (2 Cor. 5:10).

God has not spoken about many of the events that take place in heaven, but what He has said indicates it must be at this time a place of great activity. Christians who believe in the sovereignty of God accept the fact that He is able to do anything. By His command worlds came into being, and by His word the universe is sustained. Yet reason maintains such action only occurs when it is necessary. John described the descent of the Holy City—The New Jerusalem—which measured 15,000 miles square and 15,000 miles high. Faith accepts the fact that the Almighty could have created such a place in a moment. Nevertheless, if that happened, all the inhabitants of heaven would have only been witnesses applauding the act. Reason rejects that idea. God's country is filled with angels and redeemed souls who have dedicated their time and talent to the service of the Lord. It is written, "They . . . serve him day and night in his temple" (Rev. 7:15). If the events of earth resemble the activities of heaven, then God's servants are exceedingly active. Every auspicious event on this planet is preceded by great planning so that everything will be ready for the opening day. When a city is permitted to host the Olympic Games or any other international event, preparation begins years ahead of the inaugural ceremonies. Stadiums are erected, millions of dollars spent, and all kinds of decisions are made to make the occasion memorable. Maybe the same thing applies in God's country where some of the most important events are scheduled to take place.

The time is approaching when for the second time in history God's people will march into their true homeland. Paul described that event when he wrote:

> *For the Lord himself shall descend from heaven with a shout, with the voice of the archangel, and with the trump of God: and the dead in Christ shall rise first: Then we which are alive and remain shall be caught up together with them in the clouds, to meet the Lord in the air; and so shall we ever be with the Lord (1 Thess. 4:16–17).*

The Christian church has been divided in its interpretation of Paul's words. Teachers differ on the time this will take place, but they all agree *it will happen*. The dead bodies of Christians will be resurrected, and the living saints will be changed in a moment, in the twinkling of an eye, and together they will ascend to be with the returning Christ. Millions of souls will meet their Master, and for that glorious moment preparation will need to be made. Several questions could be asked.

- In addition to the Lord, by whom will the saints be met?
- Will they need nourishment, and if so, by whom will it be provided?
- Where will they be accommodated?
- How will they be clothed?
- Will they wear the long white robes which represent the righteousness of saints?
- What will be the color of our skin when we are changed in a moment; in the twinkling of an eye?
- Will it still be possible to discern that the redeemed have come from "every kindred and tongue, and people and nation"?
- Is it safe to assume that with the approach of this stupendous

event, heaven is filled with excited angels and saints as they prepare for that thrilling event?

The Bible describes how the works of the redeemed will be tried in the fires of God's scrutiny, when Christians will be rewarded for everything which they conscientiously did for the Savior.

> *For other foundation can no man lay than that is laid, which is Jesus Christ. Now if any man build upon this foundation gold, silver, precious stones, wood, hay, stubble; Every man's work shall be made manifest: for the day shall declare it, because it shall be revealed by fire; and the fire shall try every man's work of what sort it is. If any man's work abide which he hath built thereupon, he shall receive a reward. If any man's work shall be burned, he shall suffer loss: but he himself shall be saved; yet so as by fire (1 Cor. 3:11–15).*

Salvation is a gift from God, but rewards have to be earned. When a person becomes a Christian, he—so to speak—begins to work for the Heavenly Firm. His name is entered upon God's payroll, and from that moment a record is kept of his labor for the Savior. His former indiscretions are forgotten; he is given a new start. He should never worry about sins committed earlier, for God said through Jeremiah, "I will forgive their iniquity, and I will remember their sins no more" (Jer. 31:34). Christ said to the woman, "Go, and sin no more" (John 8:11). All Christians should remember those words and, "forgetting those things which are behind, and reaching forth unto those things which are before, press toward the mark for the prize of the high calling of God in Christ Jesus" (Phil. 3:13–14). The Lord also said that if a cup of cold water were given in His name, it would not pass unnoticed. God, who is able to see a sparrow falling anywhere in the world, has exceptionally good eyesight! He is aware of any dedicated service rendered to His Son.

Paul mentions two types of work done by those who profess to be Christians. He wrote of gold, silver, and precious stones and then of wood, hay, and stubble. He also indicated the obvious. The first three are imperishable; they stand the test of fire. The others do not; they are easily consumed. It was significant that the apostle emphasized an important detail. "He himself shall be saved, yet so as by fire." It is exclusively the work of Christ to get a man into the kingdom of heaven, but what position that man will occupy there is his own responsibility. Promotion has to be earned.

Students on earth anticipate "graduation day," when in the presence of an appreciative audience, they receive diplomas. At the Judgment Seat of Christ the church will reach its graduation day. If individuals remained faithful to their commitment to the Savior, they will receive in the presence of a vast audience the reward of diligence. If, on the other hand, they wasted their time, they will be denied the coveted honor, and regret and shame will follow.

It is important to remember that Jesus said, "Therefore when thou doest thine alms, do not sound a trumpet before thee, as the hypocrites do in the synagogue and in the streets, that they may have glory of men. Verily, I say unto you, *They have their reward*" (Matt. 6:2). Service done for the glory of self is not appreciated in God's presence. Anything done grudgingly never finds recognition in His hall of justice. Yet it was truly significant that the Savior saw and recognized the devotion of a widow who quietly placed into the treasury all she possessed—two mites! Probably there will be many surprises at the Judgment Seat of Christ. Important people will go away disappointed. Yet, on the other hand, some who would consider their labor to be unworthy of mention will be astonished by their crown of glory.

Where and how will this great gathering take place? Will there be a vast auditorium where at stipulated times believers will take turns appearing before the Lord? Normally, and according to earth's standards, this would take forever. God must have special equipment, for after a period of seven years the task will have been completed, and the saints will be ready to return to earth. Their assignments will already have been given. Some will rule over many cities, some over few, and others will not reign at all. These are the people of whom it is said, "But they themselves shall be saved, yet so as by fire." There are many questions we would like answered. Assuredly, throughout God's empire this event will command a great amount of attention. Even the angels will be interested to see what transpires.

The Rewards for God's Faithful Servants

It is refreshing to remember that when Simon Peter reminded the Lord of the sacrifices made by the disciples, the Savior replied, "There is no man that hath left house, or parents, or brethren, or wife, or children, for the kingdom of God's sake, Who shall not receive manifold more in this present time, and in the world to come life everlasting" (Luke 18:29–30). The Savior's final statement was thought provoking. As the old proverb suggests, "No man should count his chickens before they are hatched." Some people who expect to receive great rewards may be disappointed; others who expect nothing may be surprised and delighted. It is impossible to describe all the rewards to be bestowed upon the faithful servants of God, but it is significant that writers of the New Testament mentioned six different crowns.

(1) The Incorruptible Crown

Know ye not that they which run in a race run all, but one receiveth the prize? So run, that ye may obtain. And every man that striveth for the mastery is temperate in all things. Now they do it to obtain a corruptible crown. But we an incorruptible. I therefore so run, not as uncertainly; so fight I, not as one that beateth the air. But I keep under my body, and bring it into subjection, lest that by any means, when I have preached to others, I myself should be a castaway (1 Cor. 9:24–27).

When Paul sent this message to the Corinthians, he was evidently thinking about the sporting events in Rome. The prize was only a laurel wreath which would soon wither and die. Yet to win that prize athletes sacrificed, trained, and were subject to severe discipline. They did not wish breathlessly to beat the air. The apostle reminded his readers that Christians were striving to win an eternal crown. To do this no sacrifice should be too great, and no preparation too tedious. The prize would be "an inheritance incorruptible, and undefiled, and that fadeth not away, reserved in heaven" (1 Peter 1:4).

(2) The Crown of Rejoicing

For what is our hope, or joy, or crown of rejoicing? Are not even ye in the presence of our Lord Jesus Christ at his coming? (1 Thess. 2:19).

Evidently this reward will be given to soul winners. Paul was endeavoring to convince his converts in Thessalonica that meeting them in the presence of the Lord would surpass any other happiness in heaven. Probably John would have agreed with him, for he wrote, "I have no greater joy than to hear that my children walk in truth" (3 John 4). Daniel, who was given a special vision concerning the end times, said, "And many of them that sleep in the dust of the earth shall awake, some to everlasting life, and some to shame and everlasting contempt. And they that be wise shall shine as the brightness of the firmament; *and they that turn many to righteousness* as the stars for ever and ever" (Dan. 12:2–3). Solomon expressed true wisdom when he wrote, "He that winneth souls is wise" (Prov. 11:30).

(3) The Crown of Glory

And when the chief Shepherd shall appear, ye shall receive a crown of glory that fadeth not away (1 Peter 5:4).

When an athlete passed the finish line, watchers in the grandstands rose to applaud the achievement of the runner. Even Caesar would smile as he placed the crown upon the victor's head. As Peter visualized the scene, his thoughts went ahead to the day when the King of Kings and multitudes of redeemed souls would recognize the prowess of earth's spiritual athletes. Christ would place crowns upon the heads of winners, and the recipients would never regret the effort made to finish the race triumphantly. Paul said, "So run that ye may obtain."

(4) The Crown of Life

Blessed is the man that endureth temptation: for when he is tried, he shall receive the crown of life, which the Lord hath promised to them that love him (James 1:12).

This appears to be a special award for people who overcome temptation. It is not a reward for successful service but for dedication to Christ and His kingdom when evil challenges integrity. The Lord said to the church in Smyrna, "I know thy works, and tribulation, and poverty, (but thou art rich) and I know the blasphemy of them which say they are Jews, and are not, but are the synagogue of Satan. Fear none of those things which thou shalt suffer: behold, the devil shall cast some of you into prison, that ye may be tried; and ye shall have tribulation ten days: be thou faithful unto death, and *I will give thee a crown of life*" (Rev. 2:9–10).

(5) The Crown of Righteousness

Henceforth there is laid up for me a crown of righteousness, which the Lord, the righteous judge, shall give me at that day: and not to me only, but unto all them also that love his appearing (2 Tim. 4:8).

The apostle Paul who had preached the gospel throughout the world of his day was convinced the Lord would reward his effort. He prefaced his statement with a brief record of achievements. "For I am now ready to be offered, and the time of my departure is at hand. I have fought a good fight, I have finished my course, I have kept the faith" (2 Tim. 4:6–7). He had reached the end of his ministry and was ready to meet his Lord. There may be a connection between his testimony and the advice given to the Ephesians. They were urged to "put on the breastplate of righteousness"— something which the apostle had worn throughout his life. He whose heart had been covered by righteousness was a worthy recipient of the highest honor heaven could bestow.

(6) The Crowns of Gold

And round about the throne were four and twenty seats:
and upon the seats I saw four and twenty elders sitting,
clothed in white raiment; and they had on their heads
crowns of gold (Rev. 4:4).

When John described the scene in heaven, he emphasized two
things. The elders were clothed in white raiment, which represented the righteousness of saints (see Rev. 19:8). They had already been crowned with gold, which indicated they were *kings*
and *priests* unto God. They were greater than the Aaronic priests,
for they not only wore the breastplate of righteousness; they were
crowned with gold, a privilege never enjoyed by those who interceded for Israel.

The varying awards mentioned by the apostles represent some
of the honors to be bestowed upon the servants of Christ. It should
be remembered the Lord warned His church of the possibility of
losing one's crown (see Rev. 3:11). When the proceedings at the
Judgment Seat of Christ have been completed, the appointees
for positions of authority within the kingdom of Christ will be
ready, and probably trained, to do whatever will be necessary
when Christ reigns in Jerusalem.

A friend of mine asked a question, "Do you think we shall go
to school in heaven?" He went on to say, "If the saints are to
reign with Christ, do you think they will need special training to
be prepared for any emergency which may arise? For example,
supposing I were asked to rule over a city, or two, or ten, what
would I know about that kind of job? Surely the Lord would not
expect anyone to do something for which he was not qualified.
So there must be a place where the saints will be taught what
they need to know. Maybe the Lord has special universities where
we shall be enrolled." My friend's suggestion was at least stimulating!

When the late Conway Twitty returned to America after a two-
week concert tour of China, a crowd of his admirers gave him a
rousing welcome. An elderly lady who had been a missionary in
China for more than forty years seemed a little disappointed when

she murmured, "He was there two weeks; I was there over forty years, and yet no one is here to meet me." Then she heard God's whisper, "Ah, but you are not home yet."

Heaven's Department of Agriculture Will Be Phenomenal

And he shewed me a pure river of water of life, clear as crystal, proceeding out of the throne of God and of the Lamb. In the midst of the street of it, and on either side of the river, was there the tree of life, which bare twelve manner of fruits, and yielded her fruit every month: and the leaves of the tree were for the healing of the nations (Rev. 22:1–2).

Many years ago my wife and I were the guests of the Baptist churches of Western Australia and during our visit were sent to stay with a remarkable couple in the city of Katanning. The man was one of the pioneers who opened up the West. He shot wild dogs and tanned their skins to make his own shoes, collected empty condensed milk cans from the railway camps in the area, filled them with clay, and eventually completed a house which was made entirely of windows and the milk cans. His small vineyard was a joy to behold, but on a certain day I committed an unpardonable sin. I picked one grape from a bunch and brought upon my head the wrath of my indignant host. For a few moments I wondered if he had taken leave of his senses! He yelled, "Never do that! If you want a grape, cut a whole bunch, but never leave an empty stub on the vine; you have ruined it." It would have been easier to appreciate his anger if he sold his grapes in the market, but to do this was impossible. Everybody had as much as he! My host seemed to be unconcerned about that fact. He was a perfectionist who hated cats. With his small rifle he shot every feline that invaded his garden. I never picked a solitary grape again; I was afraid he might mistake me for a cat with two legs!

I shall always remember a morning when I discovered a strange tree. I walked around the thing several times to make sure I was not dreaming. It was filled with different kinds of oranges, grapefruit, and lemons. I was dumbfounded until my host explained that he was an expert grafter. He had inserted into the main tree small cuttings from other trees and had produced one which bore different kinds of fruit. My friend explained this could only be done with citrus, apples, and pears, or other related families such as plums, peaches, and damsons. I wish it were still possible to speak with him. He did something which I thought to be impossible, and I would like to know his opinion about a strange text in the Bible.

When John described the New Jerusalem, he mentioned a tree which bore twelve manner of fruits, and yielded its fruit every month. That appears to be absurd, but at least it supplies evidence that heaven's Ministry of Agriculture was something special. The Tree of Life was placed in the garden of Eden as a means by which Adam and Eve could gain immortality. "And the LORD God said, Behold, the man is become as one of us, to know good and evil and now, lest he put forth his hand, and take also of the tree of life, and eat, *and life for ever*: Therefore the LORD God sent him forth from the garden" (Gen. 3:22–23). When the first humans sinned, they lost their chance of receiving everlasting life. That opportunity was never forthcoming again until the Lamb of God took sins to the Cross and removed the barrier between God and man. The Tree of Life appears again in the New Jerusalem so that men and women may have the opportunity of regaining what Adam and Eve never possessed. The Bible teaches that during the reign of Christ upon earth people will live to be very old, but the end of mortality is always death—even if they live to be a thousand years of age. "The last enemy that shall be destroyed is death" (1 Cor. 15:26). The Tree of Life will be provided so that those who survive the Millennium will be able to live eternally.

This text belongs to an age beyond time, when there can be no other sickness for which nations need healing. "The leaves of the tree were for the healing of the nations" (Rev. 22:2). Nevertheless, that hardly explains the miracle in the text. It may be significant that John said: "In the midst of the street of it *and on either side of the river, was there the Tree of Life.*" It appears there were at least two trees, and they could have represented many more found in God's country. Surely this suggests that heaven's Department of Agriculture had produced something previously unknown. Will apples, oranges, cherries, and every other kind of fruit grow on one tree?

Will It Be Possible to Go Fishing in Heaven?

There was a time when this question would have been considered absurd, but now it is difficult to decide what the answer should be. Many of my friends were ardent fishermen; their happiest hours were spent waiting for a fish to tug at the line. Some of them have gone to be with the Savior, but occasionally I have heard their families saying, "I wonder if Dad has gone fishing in heaven?" This appeared to be wishful thinking, an idea not based on Scripture. The prophet Ezekiel who spoke of Christ's reign on earth, described a river which flowed from the altar of God.

> *Afterward he brought me again unto the door of the house; and, behold, waters issued out from the threshold of the house eastward: for the forefront of the house stood toward the east, and the waters came down from under from the right side of the house, at the south side of the altar (Ezek. 47:1).*

These words agree with the statement made by Zechariah:

> *And it shall be in that day, that living waters shall go out from Jerusalem; half of them toward the former sea, and half of them toward the hinder sea: in summer and in winter shall it be. And the LORD shall be king over all the earth: in that day shall there be one LORD, and his name one (Zech. 14:8–9).*

Continuing his description, Ezekiel wrote:

> *And it shall come to pass, that everything that liveth,*
> *which moveth, whithersoever the rivers shall come, shall*
> *live: and there shall be a very great multitude of fish,*
> *because these waters shall come thither: for they shall*
> *be healed; and everything shall live whither the river*
> *cometh. And it shall come to pass, that the fishers shall*
> *stand upon it from Engedi even unto Eneglaim; they*
> *[there] shall be a place to spread forth nets; their fish*
> *shall be according to their kinds, as the fish of the great*
> *sea, exceeding many (Ezek. 47:9–10).*

The prophet was convinced there would be excellent fishing during the reign of Christ. He indicated that "fishers" would stand along the banks of the rivers, and conditions would be excellent. Is it possible to identify those fishermen? There will be people over whom Christ reigns and saints who returned to earth to reign with their Lord. That they possess immortal bodies presents no problem, for even the Savior after His resurrection ate a piece of broiled fish. "And while they yet believed not for joy, and wondered, he said unto them, Have ye here any meat? And they gave him a piece of a broiled fish, and of an honeycomb. And he took it, and did eat before them" (Luke 24:41–43). These Scriptures do not describe things actually happening in heaven. One might argue that if glorified saints can fish in the river flowing from Jerusalem, why cannot they do the same in God's country?

It would be easier to answer that question if it were possible to obtain authentic information concerning a text written by Paul. He told the Corinthians that "the last enemy to be destroyed is death" (1 Cor. 15:26). God supplied animals so that they could provide food for the human race. He will do the same when fishermen stand on the banks of that marvelous river of the future. It has long been believed that the death that Paul mentioned is death that terminates life. How broad an interpretation can be given of the apostle's words? Would it include the decease of birds, animals, and fish? Following the reign of the Savior, sinners will stand before the throne of God, eternity will begin, and tragedy of any kind will be unknown. There is no evidence to prove that God, who arranged the death of animals in the old dispensations, will object to its presence in His kingdom. Yet it should be emphasized that we do not have the answers to many questions. It should be remembered, however, that God's country is not a mythical, mystical sphere of which we know nothing. The Lord provided a wonderful world in which people could live; He will do even better in His world of the future.

Jesus of Nazareth was a carpenter by trade, but throughout His life He exhibited an interest in fishing. He called fishermen to be His disciples, sent Peter to catch a special fish with a coin in its mouth, and promised to make His followers fishers of men. John supplied an interesting text.

> *As soon then as they were come to land, they saw a fire of coals there, and fish laid thereon, and bread (John 21:9).*

The Lord caught His own fish! Extremists might consider that to be a crime—that He actually killed fish! Their reasoning would be faulty, for the Bible says He was without sin. If the Lord could catch fish and remain sinless, it might be possible for the saints either here or in heaven to emulate His example.

Only One Person Wept in Heaven

> *And I saw in the right hand of him that sat on the throne a book written within and on the backside, sealed with seven seals. And I saw a strong angel proclaiming with a loud voice, Who is worthy to open the book, and to loose the seals thereof? And no man in heaven, nor in earth, neither under the earth, was able to open the book, neither to look thereon. And I wept much, because no man was found worthy to open and to read the book, neither to look thereon. And one of the elders saith unto me, Weep not: behold, the Lion of the tribe of Judah, the Root of David, hath prevailed to open the book, and to loose the seven seals thereof. And I beheld, and, lo, in the midst of the throne and of the four beasts, and in the midst of the elders, stood a Lamb as it had been slain, And he came and took the book out of the right hand of him that sat upon the throne (Rev. 5:1–7).*

When John was imprisoned upon the isle of Patmos, he was transported in spirit into the presence of God to see the things we are about to consider. Whether he had a vision or was actually carried into heaven is not important. As far as he was concerned, he actually watched the heavenly proceedings and was unable to prevent tears rolling down his face. His sorrow was uncontrollable; he was the only person to weep in the presence of Almighty God. It is important that the reason for his grief be understood.

The saints, represented by the elders, were already in heaven, and attention was focused upon a book which had seven seals. It was imperative that someone be found worthy to break the seals and read the manuscript, for the plans of the Almighty were within that volume. They referred to the redemption of God's property. The Hebrew laws applied to people and land. God gave precise instructions that if for any reason farms were sold, they returned to the original owner at the year of Jubilee. At any other time the land could be redeemed by a relative of the original owner, and people living on the property could be dispossessed. To make this valid, certain documents were required. At the time of sale there were two scrolls which related to the transaction. One was sealed; it contained specifications concerning price, and requirements for reclaiming the land. The other was signed on the back with the names of witnesses who attested to the reliability of the facts expressed therein. Without those deeds, repossession would have been extremely difficult.

When John wept in heaven, it was not because he was filled with idle curiosity and disappointed that he could not read the contents of the book. The apostle knew the significance of that scroll. He wept because he knew God's plan of redemption included the earth, an alienated property controlled by Satan. John believed God's arrangements would be spoiled if they were only half fulfilled. The angel reassured the weeping disciple that his fears were groundless. The Lion of the tribe of Judah could, and would, complete what had been commenced. He would break the seals, reveal the conditions of repossession, and bring back to its original owner the lost planet earth.[1]

This incident, so vividly described by John, was strategically placed within the book of Revelation. The history of the church was reflected in the letters sent to the assemblies in Asia (chapters 2–3). The homegoing of the church may be seen in that the elders were already seated before the throne of God (chapters 4–5). The church is not mentioned again until Christ returns to earth (chapter 19). The opening of the book with seven seals begins the period when the Redeemer proceeds with His methods of reclaiming the property which originally belonged to God. Chapters 6–19 describe how this will be done. The entire scenario suggests a great storm from which devastating waves fall upon the beaches of earth. The vials, trumpets, plagues, and seals bring continuing trouble to the nations, but when the work has been completed, the Lord intends to reclaim what is rightfully His. There are four vital facts which relate both to the world, and individuals.

(1) God Remembers
There must be a multitude of details that claim God's attention, but however crowded his schedule, He remembers what needs to be done on earth. Throughout the history of the human race He has never been too late to rescue His people! Faith in His continuing kindness is essential to happiness.

(2) God Responds
"Like as a father pitieth his children, so the LORD pitieth them that fear him" (Ps. 103:13). "Then they cry unto the LORD in their trouble, and he saveth them out of their distresses" (Ps. 107:19). This is a thrilling experience of the Christian life. Answers to prayer enrich the soul.

(3) God Redeems
This was the theme of the song heard in heaven. It subdivides into three sections. God's *Praise*, *Purpose* and *Power*. "And the number of them was ten thousand times ten thousand, and thousands of thousands, Saying with a loud voice, Worthy is the Lamb that was slain to receive power, and riches, and wisdom, and strength, and honor, and glory, and blessing" (Rev. 5:11–12). The scope of the salvation provided by the Lord defies description. The ancient writer compared himself with a beggar sitting on a dunghill (see 1 Sam. 2:8). That such men should be elevated to sit among princes could only be miraculous. Yet that is the miracle of grace, and the saints were assured they would reign upon the earth.

(4) God Reigns
This fact should never be forgotten. One's outlook may be bleak, understanding may be denied, but in spite of every adverse circumstance,

> God is still on the throne,
> And He will remember His own;
> Though trials may press us,
> And burdens distress us,
> He never forsaketh His own.
> God is still on the throne,
> And He will remember His own:
> His promise is true,
> He will not forget you,
> God is still on the throne.

The Lord has a plan for this rebellious planet, and what has been decreed will certainly come to pass. Christ—and His people—"will reign where'er the sun, does its successive journeys run, His kingdom spread from shore to shore, 'till moons shall wax and wane no more." Three major events are planned for God's country. (1) Earth is to be reclaimed; (2) the marriage of the Lamb will be celebrated, and (3) the Day of Judgment will become a reality. These occurrences are vitally linked with heaven. Whatever the daily routine within God's empire might be, there is reason to believe that at the present time heaven is a place of unceasing activity. Three special occasions are approaching, and since angels and men are involved with them all, great preparation is surely being made.

(1) The Reclamation of the Planet Earth

Thirteen chapters in the book of Revelation describe the calamities which will devastate the earth. Famines, pestilences, storms, meteorites, and other phenomena will be permitted by God and superintended by angels in the hope that men will repent. Unfortunately, even the efforts of the Lord will fail, for it is written: "And men were scorched with great heat, and blasphemed the name of God, which hath power over these plagues: and they repented not to give him glory" (Rev. 16:9). The period of time known as *Jacob's Trouble* will end when Christ and His armies return in the clouds of heaven (see Rev. 19:14). Elsewhere it is stated that four angels will do a very special work (7:1); another angel will carry the seal of the living God (7:2). Many angels around the throne will worship (7:11). Seven angels will blow their trumpets, and throughout the book of Revelation multitudes of these heavenly beings are associated with the fulfillment of God's purposes. It may be assumed these servants of God are preparing for coming events.

(2) The Marriage of the Lamb

This will be the most glittering occasion ever seen. Millions of redeemed men and women will be arrayed in white robes; these are identified with the bride of Christ (see Rev. 19:6–9). Possibly the saints of the Old Testament dispensations will be honored guests at the celebration, music will be supplied by a choir of angels, and every form of life will rejoice. It has been said that angels are glad when they see a sinner repenting. What joy will be expressed when they see millions of precious souls being united eternally with the Son of God whose death made it possible?

(3) The Great White Throne Judgment

And I saw a great white throne, and him that sat on it, from whose face the earth and the heaven fled away; and there was found no place for them. And I saw the dead, small and great, stand before God; and the books were opened: and another book was opened, which is the book of life: and the dead were judged out of those things which were written in the books, according to their works (Rev. 20:11–12).

There is a limit to the patience of God. During the life of Noah the Lord warned that His "spirit would not always strive with man" (Gen. 6:3). That became evident when the people of that generation perished. Corruption cannot be permitted to continue indefinitely. Eternity will be filled with everything commendable, but first evil must be banished, and unrepentant people will reap what they have sown. It is written that the dead will be raised, God's books opened, and sinners will be judged according to God's records. "And death and hell were cast into the lake of fire" (Rev. 20:14). It is not known what this means; perhaps the hottest flame in eternity will be the memory that Christ died for folk who spurned His offer of salvation. It is not known what occupations may be available in the hereafter, but evangelists will have to find other jobs; not even one sinner will be won for Christ when God's door of opportunity has closed.

Notes
1. J. A. Seiss, *The Apocalypse* (Grand Rapids: Kregel Publications, 1987), 112.

The New Jerusalem Will Be the Greatest City Ever Built

When the Savior was about to leave His disciples, He said:

> *Let not your heart be troubled; Ye believe in God, believe also in me. In my Father's house are many mansions: if it were not so, I would have told you. I go to prepare a place for you. And if I go and prepare a place for you, I will come again and receive you unto myself; that where I am, there ye may be also (John 14:1–3).*

Evidently the Lord had plans to erect an eternal home for His church. John enjoyed the privilege of seeing the finished product. He gave details of the great construction descending from heaven, but few people realize the magnitude of the project. The Bible states the city was 1,500 miles square and high. If it descended upon the United States of America it would cover two-thirds of the country. Its western wall would reach from Los Angeles to Vancouver in Canada, the northern wall from Vancouver to Toronto, the eastern from Toronto to Dallas in Texas, and the southern from Dallas to Los Angeles. Its height would reach areas known only to astronauts. The weight of the city would be too much for the earth to carry and it would probably interfere with the planet's rotation. There are so many mind-boggling details connected with this project; it must be the greatest problem ever to confront heaven's Department of Construction.

The New Jerusalem: A Computer's Headache

Many years ago when I was a young Christian, I had difficulty in understanding the Scripture passages which described the New Jerusalem. I believed the city would be the eternal home of the saints, but my thoughts always returned to the size of the required home. Millions of Christians, probably billions of men and women have known the saving power of God since the church was established on the Day of Pentecost! I struggled with my problem, and finally ceased to wonder how so many people could possibly live in one city.

Readers will understand my interest when I discovered that some person had fed into a computer the dimensions as supplied in Revelation 21:9–21. I am not aware of the identity of the person responsible for the following paragraph; I copied it from one of the Christian magazines published in America.

> The city itself is said to be 12,000 furlongs (1,500 miles) square. If it descended upon the earth, it would cover two thirds of the United States of America. Its walls would be 260 feet across, which is the length of a city block. They would contain 401,850 cubic feet of pure jasper. If the city were laid out into blocks 500 feet square, and if the streets were 100 feet wide, there would be 15,840 blocks to each side of the city. If each residence were 100 by 200 feet wide, or 20,000 square feet, there would be 12 residences in each block. This would total 3 billion, 10 million, 867,200 residences on the ground floor alone.

> Allowing 20 feet for each floor, the city would be 396,000 floors high. The Empire State Building is only 103 floors high. The top floor would, according to the Bible, reach to a height of 1,500 miles. If we multiply the number on the ground floor by the total floors in height, we have the fantastic total of 1 quadrillion, 192 trillion, 303 billion, 411 million, 2 hundred thousand residences. Assuming there were 10 inhabitants occupying each residence, we would have as neighbors

11 quadrillion, 923 trillion, 34 billion, 112 million inhabitants. This would be if the city were in the shape of a cube.

If, as I believe, the New Jerusalem will be in the shape of a pyramid, the number of inhabitants would be correspondingly fewer, but there would still be room to accommodate 1 million times the entire population that has ever lived on earth. Should some person exclaim, "I don't believe it," he should remember that John, describing the people he saw, said, "After this I beheld, and, lo, a great multitude, which no man could number, of all nations, and kindreds, and people, and tongues, stood before the throne, and before the Lamb, clothed with white robes, and palms in their hands; and cried with a loud voice, saying, Salvation to our God which sitteth upon the throne, and unto the Lamb" (Rev. 7:9–10).

During the course of my ministry I have traveled extensively overseas; I have visited most of the outstanding attractions offered to tourists. If I could place them all together, they would not begin to compare with the city which God has prepared for His children. Possibly it will take all eternity to explore, to see, and to enjoy what lies ahead. Yet, there is reason to believe that in spite of anything we may behold, the greatest wonder will not be found in the architecture of the eternal city, but in the fact that, to get us there, the Lord Jesus shed His precious blood. We shall know Him by the print of the nails in His hands.[1]

Who Is Building the New Jerusalem?

"Is this to be taken as a real preparation, or is it only—in a way of speaking—to express the promise of reunion more deeply? Is there some actual work of the glorified Jesus going on which amounts to a necessary preparation for His glorified people? Surely it must be so. We are not as the Pilgrim fathers who had to make their own houses, and as best they could, survive until then. It is clear that a Divine Providence made the earth ready for the children of men, and in like manner Jesus is making heaven ready. Earth was made ready for Jesus to come down and live in it—a place where Jesus and the disciples could live and work. When the disciples ascend to a higher state, all things will have been made ready." [2]

The Savior said, "I go to prepare a place for you" (John 14:2). It is easy to misinterpret His statement. When a building contractor says, "I am going to build five hundred houses," he is not stating he personally will cut floorboards, lay cement, and place every brick into position. He needs the help of plumbers, carpenters, electricians, and a host of other people who will adhere to the designs found in the blueprints of the construction. Faith might insist that by the power of His word the Lord could create the New Jerusalem in moments. Yet many people claim that when God finished Creation, *He really did finish* (see Gen. 2:3). It is doubtful whether Jehovah's creative skill was ever manifested again. Christ said He was going to prepare a place for His people, and that suggested planning, designing, and intense activity. If one man had to build a city with the dimensions as mentioned by John, he would be confronted by an impossible assignment. Since the area to be covered would be as large as two-thirds of the United States of America, where would the builder commence? It is written that the angels are ministering spirits sent forth to minister to the heirs of salvation. Is it possible that they are gladly assisting the Lord in completing the eternal home of the redeemed?

During my visits to Egypt I often stood before the great pyramids. It is not known how these were constructed, but the authorities believe many thousands of workmen toiled for years to erect the tombs for the pharaohs. My imagination was always active as I tried to visualize crowds of laborers trying to move immense stones into precise positions in the enormous structure. If angels are assisting the Savior to construct His city, it becomes easy to understand why heaven is filled with intense activity. If God designed the New Jerusalem, perhaps the Lord is superintending the construction.

Why Was So Much Wealth Displayed in the Appearance of the City?

And the building of the wall of it was of jasper: and the city was pure gold, like unto clear glass. And the foun-

dations of the wall of the city were garnished with all manner of precious stones. The first foundation was jasper; the second, sapphire; the third, a chalcedony; the fourth, an emerald; The fifth, sardonyx; the sixth, sardius; the seventh, chrysolyte; the eighth, beryl; the ninth, a topaz; the tenth, a chrysoprasus; the eleventh, a jacinth; the twelfth, an amethyst. And the twelve gates were twelve pearls; every several gate was of one pearl: and the street of the city was pure gold, as it were transparent glass (Rev. 21:18–21).

To say the least, this description is astonishing. Gold, for which men have sacrificed their lives—the most coveted treasure among nations—will be commonplace in God's city. People will walk on it; it will take the place of cement! Precious pearls, once the most valuable of adornments, will be so large that one of them will enhance the beauty of every entrance. At this point we can only speculate whether one pearl adds to the beauty of the architecture, or if the pearls are so large they adorn an entire entrance. These details emphasize the fact that the greatest valuables on earth are insignificant when compared with God's treasures. The city will be made of gold (21:18). One wonders where such vast quantities of this precious metal can be found and where all the dazzling gems may be obtained. The Lord has resources which supersede anything man can imagine. Those precious stones will be as common as pebbles on a rocky coast. An expert lapidary would probably desire to enjoy his heaven, examining the gems and gold embedded in the walls and gates of the city.

Why Did the City Have No Temple?
And I saw no temple therein: for the Lord God Almighty and the Lamb are the temple of it (Rev. 21:22).

Following the great spiritual awakening which came to Wales in the years 1904–1905, the late Rev. R. B. Jones, the minister of the Baptist Church in Porth, wrote a book called *Rent Heavens*. It vividly described many of the amazing events which occurred. He said,

"*God was everywhere,*" and emphasized the presence of the Lord filled homes, streets, mountains, valleys, cities, towns, and the entire country. People went to church services to share fellowship with other Christians, to hear magnificent singing, and to be thrilled by preachers who had met Christ. Sinners were saved, backsliders restored, saints refreshed, and it was evident *God was everywhere.*

That was a remarkable experience, but it will be insignificant when compared with what will happen in the New Jerusalem. Sanctuaries will not be found; people will never build cathedrals nor make a pilgrimage to a distant shrine. Wherever folk may be in that city, they only have to listen to hear His voice. "And the city had no need of the sun, neither of the moon, to shine in it; for the glory of God did lighten it, and the Lamb is the light thereof" (Rev. 21:23).

> *And there came unto me one of the seven angels . . . and talked with me, saying, Come hither, I will shew thee the bride, the Lamb's wife. And he carried me away in the spirit to a great and high mountain, and shewed me that great city, the holy Jerusalem, descending out of heaven from God (Rev. 21:9–10).*

How this tremendous accomplishment will be completed is unknown. The laws of gravity demand that everything falls to the earth. After years of planning, methods were discovered by which re-entry into the earth's atmosphere was made possible. Those who venture into space now expect to return safely; nevertheless, how the descent of the New Jerusalem will be controlled remains a mystery. Slowly, safely, the city will descend from heaven, and that implies a very long journey to an exact destination. John said:

> *And I saw a new heaven and a new earth: for the first heaven and the first earth were passed away; and there was no more sea. And I John saw the holy city, new Jerusalem, coming down from God out of heaven, prepared as a bride adorned for her husband. And I heard a great voice out of heaven saying, Behold, the taber-*

> *nacle of God is with men, and he will dwell with them,*
> *and they shall be his people, and God himself shall be*
> *with them, and be their God (Rev. 21:1–3).*

> *And the nations of them which are saved shall walk in*
> *the light of it: and the kings of the earth do bring their*
> *glory and honour into it. And the gates of it shall not be*
> *shut at all by day: for there shall be no night there (Rev.*
> *21:24–25).*

Evidently the new earth will be populated by a race of sinless people. These nations will be those who lived through the reign of Christ. They will have been transported from the old planet to the new. What follows remains a mystery in the mind of God. The intellect of man cannot comprehend all that He has prepared for those who love Him. Each moment of every year will be an introduction to unrivaled beauty.

> When we've been there ten thousand years,
> Bright shining as the sun,
> We've no less days to sing God's praise
> Than when we'd first begun.

Notes
1. Ivor Powell, *What in the World Will Happen Next?* (Grand Rapids: Kregel Publications, 1985),175–76.
2. "John," in *The Pulpit Commentary*, ed. Joseph Exell (Grand Rapids: Wm. B. Eerdmans Publishing Company, 1950), 17:260.

The Rainbow Is the
Prettiest Sight in Heaven

After this I looked, and behold, a door was opened in heaven: and the first voice which I heard was as it were of a trumpet talking with me which said; Come up hither, and I will shew thee things which must be hereafter. And immediately I was in the spirit: and behold, a throne was set in heaven, and one sat on the throne. And he that sat was to look upon like a jasper and a sardine stone: and there was a rainbow round about the throne, in sight like unto an emerald (Rev. 4:1–3).

A rainbow is a sign of God's love: the throne is indicative of His awesome power and judgment. When the Lord placed a rainbow round the throne He expressed a tremendous fact. God's judgments are always overshadowed by His mercy.

Many wonderful things will be seen in heaven, for the flowers, fruits, and other beautiful things from this world will be reproduced in all their magnificence. The gold and precious gems used in the building of the New Jerusalem will be a delight to see, and the honor and glory which the kings of the earth will bring into the place will make the eternal city even more wonderful. To meet the people mentioned in the Scriptures, to speak with David and Jonathan, to be introduced to the apostles of Christ, to see loved ones again, to enjoy fellowship with redeemed friends, and to worship at the Savior's feet will be a privilege and pleasure long anticipated.

Yet the gold and precious stones could never be the prettiest sight in Heaven. Many of the treasures desired on earth may lose their attractiveness, but one object of beauty will retain its charm. It would be difficult to find a person uninterested in a rainbow. Storms may darken the sky and torrential rain devastate the earth, but when a colorful bow appears over the area, onlookers know the sun is still shining. Many things may disappear from the earth, but the colorful bow will abide for ever.

The Rainbow and the Patriarch

When the waters of the flood began to subside, God said to Noah:

> *This is the token of the covenant which I make between me and you and every living creature that is with you, for perpetual generations: I do set my bow in the cloud, and it shall be for a token of a covenant between me and the earth. And it shall come to pass, when I bring a cloud over the earth, that the bow shall be seen in the cloud. And I will remember my covenant, which is between me and you and every living creature of all flesh; and the waters shall no more become a flood to destroy all flesh. And the bow shall be in the cloud:* and I will look upon it, *that I may remember the everlasting covenant between God and every living creature of all flesh that is upon the earth (Gen. 9:12–16).*

The colorful arch in the clouds was conceived in the mind of God. It was to be a sign of His promise never to repeat a particular act of judgment. It was the first time "the rainbow could be seen around the throne," but it was to appear again during the passing of time. God never desired His children to live in dread of approaching catastrophes. He wanted them to look up, for rainbows are never seen by folk who always look down! David said, "I will lift up mine eyes unto the hills, from whence cometh my help" (Ps. 121:1).

The Rainbow and the Prophet

Ezekiel was a prophet famous for visions that characterized his ministry. He saw things that contemporaries did not. He was a special man who testified of things to happen in the final days of time. Among the mental pictures that came to him was one of the Son of God. The sight was so overwhelming that he fell upon his face and worshiped. Trying to describe what he had seen, Ezekiel wrote:

> *Upon the likeness of the throne was the likeness as the appearance of a man above upon it . . . I saw as it were the appearance of fire, and it had brightness round about. As the appearance of the bow that is in the cloud in the day of rain, so was the appearance of the brightness round about.* this was the appearance of the likeness of the glory of the LORD. *And when I saw it, I fell upon my face (Ezek. 1:26–28).*

The rainbow that Noah saw in the clouds was now around the Son of God. This suggested that the mercy that had been promised would now be made possible through One around whom was the brightness of the glory of God. The period in which Ezekiel ministered was an unhappy time when the strength of heathen conquerors had overwhelmed the Hebrew slaves. Jerusalem had become a memory, and music was no longer heard in the riverside homes of the captives (Ps. 137). Yet in spite of the waywardness of the tribes, Jehovah had neither forgotten nor abandoned His covenant with Abraham. Apparently the Jews had forsaken the Lord, but He still cared for them, and the rainbow around the head of the Lord was sufficient evidence to prove God's mercy was still available. Even in those ancient days the rainbow was a most attractive sight.

The Rainbow and the Pastor

> *And immediately I was in the spirit: and, behold, a throne was set in heaven, and one sat on the throne. And he that sat was to look upon like a jasper and a sardine stone: And there was a rainbow round about the throne, in sight like unto an emerald (Rev. 4:2–3).*

John was the last of the apostles to exercise a ministry on earth; the others had rejoined their Lord. With the growth of the churches the responsibility of the aged apostle increased enormously. With Paul, John was recognized as a worthy and authentic leader. He had been with the Savior during those momentous years in Galilee; his knowledge had been gained at the Lord's feet. Perhaps it was meant to be significant that John was enabled to see the rainbow around God's throne. Jehovah was still sovereign, but His love overshadowed strength. Christ remained the King of Kings, but there were wound prints in His hands and side. Maybe the apostle was told, "John, when you speak to your friends, tell them about the rainbow, and explain that God's grace is greater than their sin."

Perhaps that explains why John was known as the "Apostle of Love." He seldom mentioned anything else. He wrote five Bible books: his gospel, three short epistles, and the book of Revelation. His theme was the matchless love of God which had been shed abroad in human hearts. Within his three short epistles, John used the word "love" thirty-eight times. The disciple who saw heaven's rainbow had experienced the love of God within his own life and committed himself to the propagation of the good news. He said, "Herein is love, not that we loved God, but that he loved us, and sent his Son to be the propitiation for our sins" (1 John 4:10).

The Rainbow and the Preacher

And I saw another mighty angel come down from heaven clothed with a cloud: and a rainbow was upon his head . . . And he had in his hand a little book . . . And the voice which I heard from heaven spake unto me again, and said, Go and take the little book which is open in the hand of the angel which standeth upon the sea and upon the earth. And I went unto the angel, and said unto him: Give me the little book. And he said unto me, Take it, and eat it up; and it shall make thy belly bitter, but it shall be in thy mouth sweet as honey . . . And he said unto me, Thou must prophesy again before many peoples, and nations, and tongues, and kings (Rev. 10:1–2, 8–11).

This reference to the angel and the little book is probably the most interesting of all. It would be informative if more of the contents of the volume were known. Books represent an author's desire to impart knowledge. The message of this book was to be "sweet to the taste, but bitter to the stomach." Was the Lord trying to tell His servant that the greatest message ever told was destined to challenge the bitter effects of sin within the human breast? Was this the first step in the soul's journey from sickness to the perfection found when Christians resemble their Lord? The question might be asked why God should be so concerned with people who were persistently obstinate? Perhaps the answer is found in the fact that God's awesome throne was surrounded by a brilliant rainbow. Peter said, "The Lord is not slack concerning his promise, as some men count slackness; but is long-suffering to us-ward, not willing that any should perish, but that all should come to repentance" (2 Peter 3:9). God's faithful servants will always be true to the contents of the little book; the theme of their message will never change. There was—and still is—a rainbow around the throne.

During my ministry in South Africa, I met several American missionaries whose testimonies thrilled my soul. Eventually I was able to visit one of their stations. My host introduced me to his colleagues. Later out in the fields we walked together, and I asked that missionary, the Rev. David B. Hall, if he would tell me more about the work of the mission. He told me of his brethren and of the great work they were all doing, and the more he talked, the more my heart warmed to my American friends. Then as we neared the mission, I paused and asked one final question, "Will you tell me what has been the most wonderful experience of your life as a missionary?" He paused, and then replied, "I think the most wonderful thing that ever happened to me was in connection with a rainbow." Astonished, I asked what he meant, and he replied, "We were on the *Zamzam* when she was sunk by a German raider." My readers will appreciate how great was my interest as I listened to his story.

"On March 20th, 1941, the *S.S. Zamzam* left New York for Suez, via Trinidad and Cape Town. She was declared a neutral ship, and of her 201 passengers 144 were missionaries of whom thirty-three were children under fourteen years of age. Twenty Protestant denominations as well as the Roman Catholic Church were represented among these missionaries. They were bound for thirteen different areas in Africa. On Thursday, April 17th, at 5:30 a.m., when the ship was still three days out of Cape Town, a German surface raider began to attack us. Fifty-five shots were fired, nine striking the vessel. We all thought we had reached the end of our lives. We tumbled out of our beds, and it soon became evident our ship was sinking. It was miraculous," Mr. Hall went on, "for although death and destruction were all around us, not one of that great party of missionaries was hurt. Many were cast into the sea, their lifeboat sinking beneath them; yet although several small children were among the number, no one was drowned.

"But let me tell you about the rainbow," Mr. Hall proceeded. "You can appreciate how fearful we were. We had heard many things about brutal enemies, and here we were at their mercy. Soon it became evident that they intended to pick us up out of the water, and as we looked nervously at the enemy raider, suddenly to our wonder we saw a glorious rainbow cover the ship. How it came, we shall never know, for there were no storm conditions. But that it was there no one could doubt, for we all saw it. God had placed His sign of mercy right over the ship. We saw it and took courage. Its radiance, its exquisite beauty warmed our hearts, and we felt the Lord was with us.

"I cannot tell you of all the details of the days that followed. I only want to add that time after time God repeated His sign to us. Eventually we were transferred to another German ship—a prison ship, the *Dresden*. There were many anxious moments for us before we were put ashore in German-occupied France. The prison ship ran the blockade of the British Navy, but every time units of the British Fleet appeared on the horizon, and sometimes when it was obvious that we had been sighted, another rainbow would appear in the sky. In fact, it was so remarkable that some of the sneering German officers at the first sight of danger said to me, 'You Bible-punchers had better go and look for your rainbow.' We were put ashore in enemy-occupied France, and later were repatriated to America, arriving back in our own country toward the end of June.

"That was the outstanding experience of my life," Mr. Hall said, in concluding his story. "I have often seen rainbows," he added, "and have known that the conditions atmospherically have accounted for them, but on certain days in the Atlantic the rainbow appeared when such seemed impossible. I cannot explain it apart from the fact that God wanted us to know He had not forgotten us. It was wonderful. When I think of all those shells coming at us, when I think of our ship going down, when I think that merchants and traders aboard were injured and yet not one of our large missionary party, I am filled with amazement."

We walked together into the mission house, and as I spoke at a meeting specially convened for the missionaries, I felt rather that I should have been sitting at their feet.

We do well to remember that God said, "This is the token of the covenant which I make between me and you and every living creature that is with you, for perpetual generations: I do set my bow in the cloud, and it shall be for a token of a covenant between me and the earth. And it shall come to pass, when I bring a cloud over the earth, that the bow shall be seen in the cloud: and I will remember my covenant, which is between me and you and every living creature of all flesh . . . The bow shall be in the cloud; and I will look upon it, that I may remember the everlasting covenant between God and every living creature of all flesh that is upon the earth."

"The bow shall be in the cloud." My missionary brother said to me, "It was wonderful. There was not a cloud in the sky, and yet the rainbow completely covered the ship. God was with us." Once more we have the same truth. The servant of God and the rainbow are fit companions!

> He cannot fail, for He is God;
> He cannot fail, He's pledged His word;
> He cannot fail, He'll see me through:
> 'Tis God with whom I have to do.[1]

Notes
1. Ivor Powell, *Black Radiance* (London: Marshall, Morgan and Scott, 1949), 70–73. See also Ivor Powell, *Bible Pinnacles* (Grand Rapids: Kregel Publications, 1985), 167–68.

Sometimes There Are Delays in Heaven's Department of Communications

And another angel came and stood at the altar, having a golden censer; and there was given unto him much incense, that he should offer it with the prayers of all saints upon the golden altar which was before the throne. And the smoke of the incense, which came with the prayers of the saints, ascended up before God out of the angel's hand (Rev. 8:3–4).

There is a vast difference between prayer and praise. When a man prays, invariably he wants something. When he praises, it is evidence he has already received what he desired. Both are vital parts of the spiritual telephone service which links the soul with God. Man has excelled in the area of communications. Our ancestors would find it difficult to believe that it is now possible to speak with astronauts flying high in the sky or put a call through to almost any place on earth and get a reply within moments. Christians have often compared the telephone service with the exercise of prayer, but there are noticeable differences between the two. It is thrilling to dial a long distance call and hear a voice answering. It should be just as wonderful to speak to our heavenly Father, but it often is not. Men do not like delays. They want an immediate response, and unfortunately, this is not always forthcoming with calls put through to heaven. Men pray, hope they have been heard, and trust their request will be granted quickly. Sometimes they are disappointed when God appears to be too busy to respond!

Was John mystified when he was told the prayers of the saints were in the shallow bowls before the altar? Moses described how Aaron was instructed to burn incense before the Lord day and night as a perpetual ordinance between Jehovah and His people (see Ex. 30:1–10). David associated this idea with his prayers and said, "Let my prayer be set forth before thee as incense; and the lifting up of my hands as the evening sacrifice" (Ps. 141:2). There was truth in the vision given to John. The prayers of the saints are not only *heard* by God—they are preserved close to His altar. They are as love letters guarded safely by a young woman awaiting the arrival of her sweetheart. It is important to remember that although the prayers of the saints may not be answered immediately, they are *never* forgotten—they rest in a golden bowl before the altar, and are as perfume ascending to delight the Lord.

> *And when he had opened the fifth seal, I saw under the altar the souls of them that were slain for the word of God, and for the testimony which they held: And they cried with a loud voice, saying, How long, O Lord, holy and true, dost thou not judge and avenge our blood on them that dwell on the earth? And white robes were given unto every one of them; and it was said unto them, that they should rest yet for a little season, until their fellowservants also and their brethren, that should be killed as they were, should be fulfilled (Rev. 6:9–11).*

This text supplies information regarding the content of the unanswered prayers. The saints were anxious to see the establishing of Christ's kingdom—when sinners on earth would answer for their atrocities—and the way prepared for the earth to be filled with the glory of God.

It is evident that when the judgments of God were being poured upon the earth, when men and women were being killed because of their allegiance to Christ, heaven's administration was busy welcoming new people to their homeland. That the newcomers were presented with white robes suggests they had already received their new bodies. It would be difficult to place garments on invisible spirits! If it is permissible to paraphrase their question, they were saying, "Lord, is it true that the kingdom is approaching when God shall wipe away all tears? Is it true there will be no more pain, sickness, nor death?" "Yes, that is true." "Then Lord, why do You not hasten the end? Why cannot the earth be judged that the coming of that day be hastened?" The Lord answered, "*Yet a little while. That day must come soon, but let the gospel be told once again. Someone might believe and each soul is of more value than the whole world.*"

Jeremiah would have applauded that answer. He wrote: "It is of the Lord's mercies that we are not consumed, because his compassions fail not. They are new every morning: great is thy faithfulness" (Lam. 3:22–23). God's love and wisdom contribute to each other's efficiency. His love guarantees prayer will be answered—His wisdom that it will happen at the right moment.

When the disciples asked the Lord to teach them how to pray, He supplied a pattern prayer that included several personal requests. Probably the most important petition was: "Thy kingdom come. Thy will be done, as in heaven, so in earth" (Luke 11:2). It was wise to pray about daily bread, forgiveness, and deliverance in time of temptation, but nothing could be as desirable as the establishing of God's kingdom upon earth. Evidently that kind of prayer would be answered—*but not immediately*! God, who sees the end from the beginning, has a precise time when that will become a reality. Meanwhile, such prayers are placed in the bowl by the altar. Prayers cannot be ignored nor forgotten; they are as incense ascending to delight the Lord. When God delays an answer to prayer, His reasons for so doing are always wise, even though His children cannot understand why an immediate response is not forthcoming. The first book of Samuel supplies an exciting example of this truth.

> *And when the time was that Elkanah offered, he gave to Peninnah his wife, and to all her sons and her daughters, portions. But unto Hannah he gave a worthy portion; for he loved Hannah: but the LORD had shut up her womb. And her adversary also provoked her sore, for to make her fret, because the LORD had shut up her*

*womb. And as he did so year by year, when she went up
to the house of the LORD, so she provoked her; therefore
she wept, and did not eat. Then said Elkanah her husband to her, Hannah, why weepest thou? and why eatest
thou not? am not I better to thee than ten sons? (1 Sam.
1:4–8).*

It was believed in those days that a childless woman was ac-
cursed by Jehovah. To be nagged each day by another jealous wife
was terrible, but the stigma of being cursed by Jehovah was a bur-
den too heavy to carry. Hannah knew she was loved by her husband, but that did not remove the ache from her heart nor destroy
the criticism of neighbors. The distracted woman prayed continu-
ously, but God appeared to be either deaf or indifferent. Every day
seemed endless; and every month an eternity to that harassed house-
wife. She prayed before the altar of God, but even that was unfortunately misunderstood by the priest who thought she was
intoxicated.

*And it came to pass, as she continued praying before
the LORD, that Eli marked her mouth. Now Hannah, she
spake in her heart; only her lips moved, but her voice
was not heard: therefore Eli thought she had been
drunken. And Eli said unto her, How long wilt thou be
drunken? Put away thy wine from thee. And Hannah
answered and said, No, my lord, I am a woman of a
sorrowful spirit; I have drunk neither wine nor strong
drink, but have poured out my soul before the Lord.
Count not thine handmaid for a daughter of Belial; for
out of the abundance of my complaint and grief have I
spoken hitherto. Then Eli answered and said: Go in
peace and the God of Israel grant thee thy petition that
thou hast asked of him (1 Sam. 1:12–17).*

Hannah desired a son more than anything else on earth, but
God listened and waited. She saw the emptiness of her life; Jehovah saw a decadent nation. Hannah sought a son; God looked for a

Savior to evangelize Israel. To use the language of John, it may be said that Hannah's prayer was placed in the golden bowl to be considered at a later date! That poor woman did not realize what was happening, but while she waited for God, He waited for her! The salvation of a nation was more important than the satisfaction of a despondent woman. Perhaps a sigh was heard in Heaven when Hannah "vowed a vow, and said, O LORD of hosts, if thou wilt indeed look on the affliction of thine handmaid, and remember me, and not forget thine handmaid, but wilt give unto thine handmaid a man child, then I will give him unto the Lord all the days of his life, and there shall no razor come upon his head" (1 Sam. 1:11).

> God moves in a mysterious way
> His wonders to perform;
> He plants His footsteps in the sea,
> And rides upon the storm.
> Deep in unfathomable mines
> Of never failing skill:
> He treasures up His bright designs
> And works His sovereign will.

"And he [Christ] spake a parable unto them to this end, that men ought *always* to pray, and not to faint" (Luke 18:1). Many people pray earnestly for a time, but when nothing happens, their enthusiasm wanes, and they begin praying about something else. Is it possible that some of our petitions need to wait in God's bowl before the altar! Perhaps our patience needs to be strengthened. One of the most rewarding texts in the epistle to the Hebrews is: "For ye have need of patience, that, after ye have done the will of God, ye might receive the promise. For yet a little while and *he that shall come will come*, and will not tarry" (Heb. 10:36–37).

The King of Heaven Will Finally Abdicate

> *Then cometh the end, when he shall have delivered up*
> *the kingdom to God, even the Father; when he shall*
> *have put down all rule and all authority and power.*
> *For he must reign, till he hath put all enemies under his*
> *feet. The last enemy that shall be destroyed is death.*
> *For he hath put all enemies under his feet. But when he*
> *saith, all things are put under him, it is manifest that he*
> *is excepted, which did put all things under him. And*
> *when all things shall be subdued unto him, then shall*
> *the Son also himself be subject unto him that put all*
> *things under him, that God may be all in all (1 Cor.*
> *15:24–28)*

Most theologians agree Paul's words are difficult to understand. The statement that the Savior will relinquish all authority and power is hard to accept, and many people ask, "Where does that leave Christ?" Some strange explanations have been offered, but it seems evident that if Paul had meant anything else, he would have said so. The apostle believed that at the end of time the Lord would deliver the kingdom into the hands of His Father, and God would become the absolute ruler of the universe.

It is important to consider the words *"then cometh the end."* There is a precise time when the events predicted by Paul will happen, and that moment is clearly revealed in the Scriptures. John believed the Lord would return to earth, be accepted by the Jewish nation, and crowned King of Kings. The Bible states He will reign for one thousand years and during that period of time, Satan will be inactive (Rev. 20:1–6). Ultimately the Devil will be released to

119

attack God's people, but that effort will be defeated when fire descends from heaven to destroy Satan and his followers. John describes how, following that catastrophe, the dead will be resurrected and judged, the New Jerusalem will descend from heaven, and time will cease as the eternal age begins. "*Then* cometh the end." Death will be abolished, the enemies of righteousness destroyed, and God's universe will be revolutionized. Upon a new earth will stand the Holy City, and the bride of Christ will be ready to occupy her eternal home.

God will be upon His throne, but the Savior will be confronted by a very important problem. Probably in the new heavens will be innumerable planets and celestial spheres. It is difficult to believe these will only be ornaments hanging in space. Surely they will fulfill some purpose and may even be inhabited. To reign over such an empire would be a great honor, and the King of Kings would be a worthy occupant of that throne. Yet Paul was assured Christ will decline the honor and gladly surrender the privilege to His Father.

Perhaps He will say, "Father, I know I am within my right to sit upon a throne of eternal splendor and be Lord of the Universe. Nevertheless, I decline that privilege. The work that was given to me I have finished, but now I wish to remain with those I redeemed."

An episode from British history may shed light on this absorbing theme. The King of England died in 1936, and the Prince of Wales succeeded to the throne. He became King Edward VIII. Unfortunately rumors began to circulate which associated the new monarch with an American woman, Mrs. Wallis Warfield Simpson. On October 22 the American newspapers began to give much space to the allegations, and the royal situation caused grave concern to the British government. After a secret meeting with Prime Minister Baldwin, the king said he intended to marry Mrs. Simpson, even if it meant abdication. He later spoke by radio to the nation and said: "I have found it impossible to discharge my duties as king, as I would wish to do, without the help and support of the woman I love." He abdicated and thereafter spent his life with the woman for whom he sacrificed a throne.

From several angles that illustration from British history is a poor comparison with the event described by Paul. The bride of Christ for whom an eternal throne will be forfeited will be holy and without blemish. Clothed in a white robe, she will be resplendent with beauty; her righteousness will be untarnished. There will not be any stain upon her character. The choice confronting the King of Kings will be important. Either He can occupy a throne of scintillating brilliance, or He can refuse that opportunity and marry the church. When Christ renounces His throne in favor of His bride, even the angels might hold their breath as heaven is filled with adoration and praise. After the Lord has placed His crown at the feet of His Father, the bride and Groom will commence their everlasting honeymoon in the greatest vacation city ever built.

A Bunch of Everlastings!

And they came unto the brook of Eschol, and cut down from thence a branch with one cluster of grapes, and they bare it between two upon a staff; and they brought of the pomegranates, and of the figs (Num. 13:23).

The children of Israel had never been in Canaan, and it was understandable why they should desire information regarding the land they were expected to occupy. The Bible describes how spies were sent to ascertain what would be necessary to conquer the territory. The men were astonished by the productivity of the country but appalled by the size of its citizens. Their message to the children of Israel was frightening, but the size of one bunch of grapes proved their report was accurate. Two of them had carried a bunch of grapes back to Israel, but even the fruit could not overcome the fear of the Hebrews.

Bible students know that Canaan was not a type of heaven. Christians do not have to expel enemies before they can enter their homeland. The Promised Land was a foreshadowing of the life in heavenly places where, according to Paul, believers wrestle "against principalities, against powers, against the rulers of the darkness of this world, against spiritual wickedness in high places" (Eph. 6:12).

Israel was given a wonderful view of the magnificent fruit to be found in Canaan. It may be suggested that the same kind of thing was made evident in the writings of the prophets and apostles. Those dedicated men were given a special view of things which lay beyond this world, and they revealed what we may expect to find in God's country. Those inspired authors, having entered by faith into the Promised Land, came back with a bunch of everlastings.

(1) The Everlasting Covenant . . . How Safe

And the bow shall be in the cloud; and I will look upon it, that I may remember the everlasting covenant between God and every living creature of all flesh that is upon the earth (Gen. 9:16).

Strong's Concordance lists fourteen Scriptures where God emphasizes that His covenant with man is eternal. When other promises concerning Israel are added to the list, the number becomes greater. The promise is not for a limited period; it is forever. It cannot be abrogated, changed, or ignored. He who has been our help in ages past, will be our hope for years to come. "He cannot fail; for He is God. He cannot fail; He's pledged His word."

(2) The Everlasting Remembrance . . . How Special

A good man sheweth favour, and lendeth: he will guide his affairs with discretion. Surely he shall not be moved for ever: the righteous shall be in everlasting remembrance (Ps. 112:5–6).

No person wishes to be forgotten by his friends, and intelligent people do not desire to be forsaken by God. The psalmist said: "I have been young, and now am old; yet have I not seen the righteous forsaken, nor his seed begging bread" (Ps. 37:25). David's observations were limited to a lifetime, but righteous people are remembered not only in time, but also in eternity. An outstanding example of this truth is found in Matthew's gospel. "And the King shall answer and say unto them, Verily I say unto you, Inasmuch as ye have done it unto one of the least of these my brethren, ye have done it unto me" (Matt. 25:40).

(3) The Everlasting Foundation . . . How Solid

As the whirlwind passeth, so is the wicked no more: but the righteous is an everlasting foundation (Prov. 10:25).

The text can be interpreted in two ways. A whirlwind lasts for a short period of time and then subsides. On the other hand, a righteous man does not disappear; he abides, and his example is a good foundation upon which neighbors can build their lives. His works are not temporary; they endure. The Lord illustrated this truth when he spoke of a man whose house survived a tempest because it was built upon a rock. The second interpretation suggests the righteous man himself is built upon a solid foundation. Paul said, "For other foundation can no man lay than that is laid, which is Jesus Christ" (1 Cor. 3:11).

(4) The Everlasting Sign . . . How Splendid

Instead of the thorn shall come up the fir tree, and instead of the brier shall come up the myrtle tree: and it shall be to the LORD for a name, for an everlasting sign that shall not be cut off (Isa. 55:13).

The prophets often mentioned signs which would precede future events. The shepherds at Bethlehem were told: "And this shall be a sign unto you; Ye shall find the babe wrapped in swaddling clothes, lying in a manger" (Luke 2:12). That sign only lasted for a short period of time. The sign mentioned by Isaiah referred to the last days, when everything which caused pain will disappear. The desert will blossom as the rose, and God's benediction will make the earth a paradise. Even through eternity this sign of God's providence will speak of the faithfulness of the Almighty.

(5) The Everlasting Possession . . . How Secure

And I will give unto thee, and to thy seed after thee, the land wherein thou art a stranger; all the land of Canaan,

*for an everlasting possession; and I will be their God
(Gen. 17:8).*

God promised Abraham that his seed would inherit Canaan
forever. At the time they were strangers in a foreign land, but the
Almighty made a tremendous commitment which has never been
changed. Although the Hebrews displeased the Lord and were
consequently scattered around the earth, they have been preserved
and restored to their rightful heritage. Enemies tried repeatedly
to expel them, but every attempt failed. Efforts are now being
made to make a peace treaty between the Jews and the Arabs, for
both parties are beginning to realize it is better to live together
peacefully than to die fighting. The fact that Palestine or Israel
will always belong to the Jews was finalized when God promised Canaan should be Israel's everlasting possession.

(6) The Everlasting Way . . . How Sanctified
*Search me, O God, and know my heart: try me, and
know my thoughts. And see if there be any wicked way
in me, and lead me in the way everlasting (Ps. 139:23–
24).*

Psalm 139 supplies evidence that David could neither escape
from God nor himself. The consciousness of sin was a continual
annoyance which filled him with frustration. He said, "Whither
shall I go from thy spirit? or whither shall I flee from thy presence? If I ascend up into heaven, thou art there: If I make my bed
in hell, behold, thou art there. If I take the wings of the morning,
and dwell in the uttermost part of the sea; even there shall thy
hand lead me, and thy right hand shall hold me" (Ps. 139:7–10).
David was being pursued by the Lord, but in all these experiences
he recognized there was an everlasting way to the heart of God.

(7) The Everlasting Salvation . . . How Satisfying
*But Israel shall be saved in the LORD with an everlast-
ing salvation: ye shall not be ashamed nor confounded
world without end (Isa. 45:17).*

Neither by the blood of goats and calves, but by his own blood he entered in once into the holy place, having obtained eternal redemption for us (Heb. 9:12).

Israel has always been a troubled nation. Famine, pestilence, and war devastated the land, and Isaiah could only have been inspired when he wrote: "Thus saith the LORD, The labour of Egypt, and merchandise of Ethiopia and of the Sabeans, men of stature, shall come over unto thee, and they shall be thine: they shall come after thee; in chains they shall come over, and they shall fall down unto thee, they shall make supplication unto thee, saying, Surely God is in thee; there is none else, there is no [other] God . . . Israel shall be saved in the LORD with an everlasting salvation" (Isa. 45:14–17). The survival of the Israelis has been a miracle and a foreshadowing of things to come. It is written that Christ obtained eternal redemption for His followers (see Heb. 9:12).

(8) The Everlasting Life . . . How Sublime

For God so loved the world, that he gave his only begotten Son, that whosoever believeth in him, should not perish, but have everlasting life (John 3:16).

Men have always believed in a life beyond the grave, but only Jesus of Nazareth claimed to be able to give it to undeserving people. That made Him unique, the most sensational preacher ever heard. The Indian tribes believe in the existence of a happy hunting ground; and the worshipers in the temples of India believe in Nirvana, a sphere, time, or place where the human spirit is absorbed into the Great Spirit, and the cares and problems of this world are banished for ever. Holy men remain motionless for long periods of time, endeavoring to prepare themselves for the moment when that experience becomes possible. They desire to isolate themselves from the world and everything associated with it. The Savior was different. He embraced children, met outcasts, and helped the needy. He not only believed in the possibility of eternal life in heaven, He enjoyed it here and said, "I am the resurrection and the life: he that believeth in me, though he were dead, yet shall he live: And whosoever liveth and believeth in me shall never die" (John 11:25–26).

(9) The Everlasting Light . . . How Scintillating
Thy sun shall no more go down; neither shall thy moon withdraw itself: for the LORD shall be thine everlasting light, and the days of thy mourning shall be ended (Isaiah 60:20).

The prophet said, "The people that walked in darkness have seen a great light: they that dwell in the land of the shadow of death, upon them hath the light shined" (Isa. 9:2). Isaiah was aware that God's light could shine in the hearts of people. It may be significant that when John described the New Jerusalem, he said there would be no light from the sun and moon for "The Lamb is the light thereof" (see Rev. 21:23). The saints will never walk in darkness for the Lord will be their everlasting light. The redeemed will never again be in darkness, for they will remain in the Lord's presence. Light and darkness cannot exist together.

(10) The Everlasting Love . . . How Surviving
The LORD hath appeared of old unto me, saying, Yea, I have loved thee with an everlasting love: therefore with lovingkindness have I drawn thee (Jer. 31:3).

The love existing between human beings is often subject to change. Words spoken in marriages are often a sham; what is promised "till death do us part" sometimes dies within months. Human affections can be fervent, frail, or forgetful. The church at Ephesus was known to be one of the greatest of its generation, but when the Lord sent His letter, He said, "I have somewhat against thee, because thou hast left thy first love" (Rev. 2:4). The Savior is able to kindle fire of devotion in the hearts of His people, but afterward each individual is responsible for its continuance. God lit the fire on the altar within the tabernacle and the temple, but the priests were informed they were expected to keep the fire burning.

Christians have neglected to do this, and therefore what should have been a wonderful fire became ashes. The poet was correct when he wrote:

> Great is Thy faithfulness, O God my Father,
> There is no shadow of turning with Thee;
> *Thou changest not,*
> *Thy compassions they fail not,*
> As Thou hast been, Thou forever wilt be.

(11) The Everlasting Joy . . . How Superb
And the ransomed of the LORD shall return, and come to Zion with songs and everlasting joy upon their heads: they shall obtain joy and gladness, and sorrow and sighing shall flee away (Isa. 35:10).

Joy is the hallmark of the Christian life; it is found in the hearts of people who have been ransomed by the Lord. When the prophet described the return of Israel from captivity, his message became entrancing. He wrote of the days spent in Babylon, and said, "By the rivers of Babylon, there we sat down, we wept, when we remembered Zion. We hanged our harps upon the willows in the midst thereof. For there they that carried us away captive required of us a song; and they that wasted us required of us mirth, saying, Sing us one of the songs of Zion. How shall we sing the LORD'S song in a strange land?" (Ps. 137:1–4). When those people returned to their homeland, their songs of praise continued, and they exclaimed, "We were like them that dream. Then was our mouth filled with laughter, and our tongue with singing: then said they among the heathen, The LORD hath done great things for them" (Ps. 126:1–2).

(12) The Everlasting Mercy . . . How Stupendous
For the LORD is good; his mercy is everlasting; and his truth endureth to all generations (Ps. 100:5).

Defining mercy, *Webster's Dictionary* says it means: "Kindness in excess of what might be expected or demanded by fairness, forbearance, and compassion." It suggests a powerful agency which has been offended, but which refuses to execute judgment. When the Savior and Simon Peter were discussing forgiveness, the disciple asked if he should forgive an offending brother "seven times." He was told to do it "seventy times seven." Probably Jesus knew it would be easier to keep on forgiving! Yet, even then there was a limit to the number of times suggested by the Lord. His mercy is everlasting; apparently, He keeps on forgiving His people! God's patience is endless.

(13) The Everlasting Righteousness . . . How Saintly
Thy righteousness is an everlasting righteousness, and thy law is the truth (Ps. 119:142).

Righteousness is a treasure beyond the purchasing power of money. It speaks of inward purity and outward dependability in all moral and spiritual issues; it never deviates from the paths of holiness. The psalmist had been associated with many people whose moral standards were deplorable, and he had not always been completely dedicated. Nevertheless, his faith in the righteousness of God remained unshaken. James said: "Every good gift and every perfect gift is from above, and cometh down from the Father of lights, *with whom is no variableness*, neither shadow of turning" (James 1:17). God is never moved by impulses nor upset by moods. His righteousness is unchanging!

(14) The Everlasting Strength . . . How Sustaining
Thou wilt keep him in perfect peace, whose mind is stayed on thee: because he trusteth in thee. Trust ye in the Lord for ever: for in the Lord JEHOVAH is everlasting strength (Isa. 26:3–4).

One of the most charming messages delivered by the Savior concerned sheep. He spoke of thieves, hirelings, robbers, and many other enemies which threatened the safety of the flock and warned His listeners of dangers that would confront them. Yet in the midst of His profound statements Jesus said, "My sheep hear my voice, and I know them, and they follow me: And I give unto them eternal life; and they shall never perish, neither shall any man pluck them out of *my hand*. My Father, which gave them me, is greater than all; and no man is able to pluck them out of *my Father's hand*" (John 10:27–29). The Lord said God's sheep are held in a dual grip. He and His Father are responsible for the safety of the sheep.

(15) The Everlasting Kindness . . . How Suggestive

For a small moment have I forsaken thee; but with great mercies will I gather thee. In a little wrath I hid my face from thee for a moment; but with everlasting kindness will I have mercy on thee, saith the LORD thy Redeemer (Isa. 54:7–8).

Kindness is attractive. A man enriches himself when he contributes to the happiness of others. God revealed His great love when He said, "For the mountains shall depart, and the hills be removed; but my kindness shall not depart from thee, neither shall the covenant of my peace be removed, saith the LORD that hath mercy on thee" (Isa. 54:10). There is a contrast in God's statement: "I hid my face from thee for *a moment* but with *everlasting* kindness will I have mercy on thee" (Isa. 54:8). Paul was correct when he wrote: "For I reckon that the sufferings of this present time are not worthy to be compared with the glory which shall be revealed in us" (Rom. 8:18).

(16) The Everlasting Consolation . . . How Soothing

Therefore, brethren stand fast, and hold the traditions which ye have been taught, whether by word, or our epistle. Now the Lord Jesus Christ himself, and God, even our Father, which hath loved us, and hath given us everlasting consolation and good hope through grace, Comfort your hearts, and stablish you in every good word and work (2 Thess. 2:15–17).

After considering the majestic attributes of the Lord, it almost seems a let-down when Paul reminds us of the sober realities of

everyday living. He told his readers it was necessary to *stand fast.*
Storms may threaten the believer and adverse circumstances interfere with his happiness, but everlasting consolation is always
available. It is frequently difficult to understand why certain things
are permitted to happen, but true faith always looks steadfastly
toward the Lord. We may not understand the reason for God's ac-
tions, but at least we can say with Job "Though he slay me, yet
will I trust in him" (Job 13:15). The surface of life's sea may be
very turbulent, but deep in the human heart there can be a peace
beyond understanding.

(17) The Everlasting Dominion . . . How Spreading

*At the end of the day, I Nebuchadnezzar lifted up mine
eyes unto heaven, and mine understanding returned unto
me, and I blessed the most High, and I praised and
honoured him that liveth for ever, whose dominion is
an everlasting dominion, and his kingdom is from generation to generation (Dan. 4:34).*

Nebuchadnezzar and other potentates of his generation were
inclined to believe they were divine. Enemies were ruthlessly sub-
dued and humiliated. Yet, even those monarchs realized their kingdoms would end, for even kings died! The account of this ruler's
acknowledgment of Jehovah makes excellent reading. He said, "Is
not this great Babylon, that I have built for the house of the kingdom by the might of my power, and for the honor of my majesty?
While the word was in the king's mouth, there fell a voice from
heaven, saying, O king Nebuchadnezzar, to thee it is spoken, Thy
kingdom is departed from thee. And they shall drive thee from
men, and thy dwelling shall be with the beasts of the field: they
shall make thee to eat grass as oxen" (Dan. 4:30–32). Nebuchadnezzar never began his relationship with Jehovah until he
ceased worshiping at his own shrine. Then he realized the divine
kingdom, unlike his own, was endless. It would spread from shore
to shore; it would never die.

(18) The Everlasting Kingdom . . . How Significant
Thy kingdom is an everlasting kingdom, and thy dominion
endureth throughout all generations (Ps. 145:13).

David and Nebuchadnezzar would have understood each other's point of view. They were vastly different and yet had much in common. The king of Israel was a warrior who had witnessed the rise and fall of many nations. He had known insurrection within his own family and had been forced temporarily into exile. When he considered earthly kingdoms, he recognized the indestructibility of God's domain which would extend to all generations. The Bible teaches that all Bible highways lead to the Savior. "In the beginning God" and in the end, the Lord Jesus Christ. "The grace of our Lord Jesus Christ be with you all. Amen" (Rev. 22:11). Happy and safe is the individual whose citizenship is in heaven (see Phil. 3:20).

(19) The Everlasting Father . . . How Sensational
For unto us a child is born, unto us a son is given: and
the government shall be upon his shoulder: and his name
shall be called Wonderful, Counseller, The mighty God,
the everlasting Father, *The Prince of Peace (Isa. 9:6).*

This statement was probably one of the prophet's most important utterances. He said the Messiah would be called *the everlasting Father*. This supports the claim that Jesus of Nazareth was equal with God. Prior to the arrival of Christ, Jehovah was not recognized as a Father. Israel believed Him to be an austere God who could be very displeased with offenders. Yet when the disciples asked to be taught how to pray, Jesus instructed them to say, "Our Father." When the Lord was about to ascend into heaven, He said to His friends: "I ascend unto my Father, *and your Father*; and to my God, and your God" (John 20:17). That approach to Jehovah was warm, inviting, and comforting. A parent can care for a child; an idol cannot. It is thrilling to know that even in eternity, God will retain that title. He will never change. The Savior remains "the same yesterday, and today, and forever" (Heb. 13:8).

It is fitting that this fact should conclude the study on "A Bunch of Everlastings." Christ is the eternal diamond with many facets. "He is altogether lovely" (Song of Sol. 5:16).

It Will Be Easy to Recognize Christ in Heaven

We shall see him as he is (1 John 3:2).

The story has often been told that after the death of a Sunday school teacher, one of her scholars, a little girl, dreamed she had gone to heaven where her friend introduced her to many celebrities. Later, when the child awakened, she reiterated her experiences, saying, "My teacher introduced me to David, and Abraham, and Paul, and a lot of other nice people." Her mother asked, "Did she not introduce you to Jesus?" "Oh, no," was the prompt reply, "I knew Jesus as soon as I saw Him. I did not need an introduction to Him."

The testimony of that child might express great truth. Heaven will be filled with many delightful people, and some of the joys to be known in eternity may be related to our meeting with new and old friends. Yet however amazing that may be, nothing will compare with the moment when we shall first see the Savior. Charles H. Gabriel was correct when he wrote:

Oh that will be glory for me, glory for me, glory for me.
When by His grace I shall look on His face,
That will be glory, be glory for me.

We Shall Know Him by His Radiant Face . . . How Glorious
And they shall see his face (Rev. 22:4).

The church has always wished the early Christians had possessed cameras, for they would have bequeathed to later generations

133

authentic pictures of the Savior. Artists have tried to produce a likeness of the Lord, but some of their ideas were expressed in crude forms. On the other hand, I remember seeing a painting on which the Savior was seen playing tug-of-war with children of several nationalities. Boys and girls from Africa, China, and Europe were pulling hard on their end of a rope, while at the other was the Savior, evidently enjoying the contest. His eyes were sparkling, His face radiant as He saw the children desperately trying to win the contest. The Lord's image was the product of a very gifted artist. There are drawings and paintings which depict every phase of the life of Jesus, but unfortunately, there is not one authentic portrait.

That could possibly be a blessing in disguise, for if there were one true picture of the Lord, it might be in a museum or made an object of unlawful veneration. Perhaps God arranged that photography would be an undiscovered art until it would no longer provide threats to legitimate worship. Maybe the Lord desired the minds of men and women to become as canvas so that each individual would be able to paint his own portrait of the Savior. It is not too difficult to imagine what John thought when he wrote, "And they shall see his face." He was excited when he described the home-going of the saints. He had already written, "That which was from the beginning, which we have heard, which we have seen with our eyes, which we have looked upon, and our hands have handled, of the Word of life; (For the life was manifested, and we have seen it . . . That which we have seen and heard declare we unto you)" (1 John 1:1–3). After writing this message to his friends, he considered the future and wrote, "And they shall see his face." That first glimpse of the Redeemer will provide thrills which will never be forgotten.

We Shall Know Him by the Tone of His Voice . . . How Gentle

My beloved spake, and said unto me, Rise up, my love;
my fair one, and come away (Song of Sol. 2:10).

The Song of Solomon is one of the most challenging books in the Bible. For centuries theologians considered it to be the story of a romance which existed between Solomon and one of his female companions. That interpretation has now been challenged by expositors who believe the letters relate to two men who loved the same girl. One was Solomon who became a victim of his own lust; the other was a shepherd, a former sweetheart. The girl undoubtedly was Abishag the Shunammite, who helped David during the closing days of his life (see 1 Kings 1:1–4). She left her home to respond to an appeal issued from the royal palace. Her charming presence caused serious repercussions, for apparently men were attracted by her personality. Prince Adonijah aroused the anger of Solomon when he sought permission to marry her (see 1 Kings 2:13–24). The Song of Solomon is now believed to be a collection of letters which suggests how the prince of this world tries to woo the church, and how the good Shepherd desires to reclaim a lost sweetheart. The young woman finally yielded to his entreaty, and even the king was fascinated by the romance.

Some of the most fascinating details of the story tell how the girl said: "My beloved spake, and said unto me, Rise up my love; my fair one, and come away" (Song of Sol. 2:10). The account became illuminating when she said: "I sleep, but my heart waketh: it is the voice of my beloved that knocketh, saying, Open to me, my sister." She did not wish to yield easily and replied: "I have put off my coat; how shall I put it on? I have washed my feet; how shall I defile them? My beloved put in his hand by the hole of the door, and my inmost being was moved for him. I rose up to open to my beloved . . . I opened to my beloved; but my beloved had withdrawn himself, and was gone: my soul failed when he spake: I sought him, but I could not find him; I called him, but he gave me no answer" (Song of Sol. 5:2–6).

It is not difficult to believe the ancient record reminds readers of The Good Shepherd and His bride-to-be. If it were possible to hear a recording of the Savior's voice, that record or tape would be the most valuable treasure in the world. When the Lord spoke in the cemetery at Bethany, His command brought Lazarus from the sepulchre. When he called Mary at the garden tomb, her doubts and fears were replaced by inexpressible joy. Some day the Lord will welcome His Bride into the glory of heaven, and we shall know Him by the gentleness of His voice. Even the officials of the law were charmed by the message of Jesus and said: "Never man spake like this man" (John 7:46).

We Shall Know Him by the Nailprints in His Hands . . . How Glorified

And one shall say unto him, What are these wounds in thine hands? Then he shall answer, Those with which I was wounded in the house of my friends (Zech. 13:6).

The Bible teaches that Christ will return to the Mount of Olives where the Israeli nation will accept Him as their Messiah, and thereafter He will reign upon the earth for one thousand years. His appearance will terminate the Battle of Armageddon, when He will stand upon the mount and hold out His arms. Someone will ask how the nailprints came to be in his hands, and the reply will bring conviction to the troubled people. They will confess their guilt and accept Him as the long awaited Messiah. That fact is remarkable, for they will be the only blemishes in the eternal state. Cripples will have inherited immortality and for the first time will enjoy living in perfect bodies. Sickness of every kind will be banished, and people who lost limbs on earth will receive replacements. Throughout the universal domain of the King of Kings there will be no imperfections. The one outstanding exception will be the Lord, for in His hands will be reminders of the price paid to save His people. The anthems sung by heaven's choir will amplify that message. "Worthy is the Lamb that was slain." It is written that God shall wipe away all tears from the eyes of His people, but it may be difficult for the redeemed to see His wound prints and not shed tears of gratitude.

We Shall Know Him by His Immortal Body . . . How Glowing

The Saviour, the Lord Jesus Christ: Who shall change our vile body that it may be fashioned like unto His glorious body, *according to the working whereby he is able even to subdue all things unto himself (Phil. 3:20–21).*

It is interesting that Paul described his body as "vile." The human frame is a remarkable mechanism which only the power of God could produce. The best robot cannot compare with the handiwork of the Almighty. That the apostle described it as being vile suggests he was more concerned with what had happened to it than with what God meant it to be.

It is believed Paul suffered from impaired vision—that this was a source of irritation when his poor eyesight restricted activities. The apostle also said that within him "dwelleth no good thing" (see Rom. 7:15–20). He recognized that within his body were inclinations to sin; that it was continually necessary to strive against the world, the flesh, and the devil. He confessed he was not always successful and passed sentence upon himself, saying, "O wretched man that I am, who shall deliver me from this body of death?" He supplied the answer to his own question: "I thank God through Jesus Christ our Lord." His message to the Philippians predicted he would be changed into the likeness of Christ's glorious body. It is easy to believe that when this happens, Paul will joyfully exclaim, "Thank God—at last!"

It is difficult to describe what those new bodies will mean to the redeemed church. The angels who were also clothed with immortality were said to be shining ones, and at His transfiguration the Lord's "face did shine as the sun, and his raiment was white as the light" (Matt. 17:2). Aches, pains, and diseases will never again threaten the health of God's people. Cancer will cease to be a menace, and Christian doctors will never be asked to minister to sick people. There will not be any hospitals nor eventide homes for the aged. All the citizens of heaven will be eternally young. "We shall be like him." Our bodies will reflect the glory of the Son of God—the Lamb upon His throne. Even to see Him will remind everybody that without divine grace admittance to God's kingdom would have been denied.

We Shall Know Him by His Resplendent Followers . . . How Great

And the armies which were in heaven followed him upon white horses (Rev. 19:14).

Special parades have always been attractive; even in ancient times when David and his soldiers brought the ark back to Jerusalem, crowds of excited people lined the streets. Glittering processions have always interested multitudes of viewers, and today such events are televised around the world. When John was imprisoned upon the isle of Patmos, God allowed him to see the greatest parade ever arranged. He saw the armies of heaven riding upon white horses and clad in shining garments. The amazing display of the military power was almost beyond comprehension as armies returned to earth to terminate the Battle of Armageddon. The soldiers of God were resplendent as they proceeded along streets of gold.

When Simon Peter prepared to defend the Lord, Jesus said, "Thinkest thou that I cannot now pray to my Father, and he shall presently give me more than twelve legions of angels?" (Matt. 26:53). The parade of God's armies provides a background to the claim made by Jesus. When Elisha's servant was petrified with fear, God opened his eyes to see soldiers of heaven were already present to defend the prophet (see 2 Kings 6:15–17). It will be easy to recognize the Lord, for He will be leading the heavenly procession. It is thrilling to remember that He who held children in His arms, will be the Commander-in-Chief of the heavenly host. He who invited people to come for rest (Matt. 11:28) will determine the eternal destiny of guilty people. It is wiser to accept Him as a friend in this world than to face Him as a judge in the next. That His garments were stained as it were with blood (Rev. 19:13) suggests that even throughout eternity we shall be reminded of the price paid for our redemption.

We Shall Know Him by His Thrilling Titles . . . God-Given

And he hath on his vesture and on his thigh a name written, KING OF KINGS, AND LORD OF LORDS (Rev. 19:16).

The titles mentioned by John were the most all-inclusive ever given to the Savior. It should be remembered that Jesus of Nazareth was always a king. Upon earth He was clothed with the garments of flesh, but that could never change the fact that He was, and remains, the greatest sovereign the universe ever knew.

The title "King of Kings" is probably the most majestic and comprehensive of all the names given to Christ. Its glory and splendor extend throughout many areas. The wise men who came to Bethlehem called Jesus the "King of the Jews" (Matt. 2:2), a title possibly associated with the title "Messiah." When Nathaniel came to Jesus, he exclaimed, "Thou art the King of Israel" (John 1:49). John, describing what he saw in heaven, addressed the Lord as "thou King of saints" (Rev. 15:3). When the writer to the Hebrews compared the Lord with Melchizedek, he explained that Christ was a priest of the same order, a royal priest, and was "the King of peace" (Heb. 7:2). David expressed his thoughts in another way when he wrote: "Lift up ye heads, O ye gates . . . and *the King of glory* shall come in" (Ps. 24:7). If Christ be *the King of Glory* and the *King of heaven* (Dan. 4:37), then He is indisputably the *King of angels* (see Heb. 1:6–8).[1]

What will take place in God's country has not been completely revealed. What we shall do and how we shall spend our time are some of God's secrets. Nevertheless kings are associated with honor, power, glory, and government. A royal family is always given a great welcome by their subjects, and every appearance in public is always a cause for excitement. There is no way of knowing if parades take place in heaven, or if scientific exploration of myriads of planets will occupy the attention of God's children. It must be evident that the Almighty did not create the heavenly spheres to hang as gigantic lanterns in space. If such endeavors are on the divine program, there will be sufficient adventure to last for ever!

There have been innumerable kings and queens during the history of mankind, and some of them had enough wisdom to lay their crowns at the Savior's feet. Their diadems were made of gold and precious stones. There will be other crowns to reward faithful saints for meritorious service. Perhaps these will be offered to the King of Kings whose grace exceeded everything every known. There may be occasions when the Savior will appear on streets of gold, when angelic hosts will acclaim His presence. Perhaps we shall share extended vacations throughout His vast domain, but one thing is certain, the redeemed of the Lord will not sit forever playing harps! Heaven will be filled with surprises, but nothing will compare with the thrill of beholding the print of the nails in His hands. Ira D. Sankey was inspired when he sang:

> When my life's work is ended, and I cross the swelling tide;
> When that bright and glorious morning I shall see,
> I shall know my Redeemer when I reach the other side,
> And His smile will be the first to welcome me.
> I shall know Him; I shall know Him;
> When redeemed by His side I shall stand:
> I shall know Him; I shall know Him,
> By the print of the nails in His hand.

Notes
1. Ivor Powell, *Bible Names of Christ* (Grand Rapids: Kregel Publications, 1988), 165.

Bibliography

Barclay, William. *The Daily Study Bible*. Philadelphia: Westminster Press, 1976.

Exell, Joseph, ed. *Pulpit Commentary*. Grand Rapids, Michigan: Eerdmans Publishing Company, 1950.

Funk and Wagnall's *Encyclopedia*. New York: , 1953.

Powell, Ivor. *Bible Highways*. Grand Rapids, Michigan: Kregel Publications, 1959.

_____ . *Bible Names of Christ*. Grand Rapids, Michigan: Kregel Publications, 1988.

_____ . *Black Radiance*. London: Marshall, Morgan and Scott, 1949.

_____ . *John's Wonderful Gospel*. Grand Rapids, Michigan: Kregel Publications, 1983.

_____ . *We Saw It Happen*. London: Marshall, Morgan and Scott, 1948.

_____ . *What in the World Will Happen Next?* Grand Rapids, Michigan: Kregel Publications, 1973.

Tan, Paul Lee. *7,700 Illustrations*. Rockville, Maryland: Assurance Publishers, 1988.

Books by Ivor Powell

Bible Cameos
Vivid biographies of 80 Bible characters graphically portrayed. Full of helps and hints for sermon preparation.
ISBN 0-8254-3515-3 **192 pp.** **paperback**

Bible Gems
Preachers will enjoy an ample supply of sermon starters, teachers will find many illustrations, and laymen will be led to the deep truths of God's Word as Powell traces 80 various Bible themes.
ISBN 0-8254-3527-7 **176 pp.** **paperback**

Bible Highways
This volume transports the reader through a variety of over 40 themes found in the Scriptures and then provides over 90 rich illustrations to communicate the message effectively. Valuable material for the pastor or teacher in a pulpit or teaching ministry.
ISBN 0-8254-3521-8 **176 pp.** **paperback**

Bible Nuggets
These 34 insightful studies of Bible characters provide enjoyable and challenging reading for pastors and teachers alike.
ISBN 0-8254-3512-9 **192 pp.** **paperback**

Bible Oases
The author provides the pastor, Bible student and Christian reader with insightful looks at "less popular portions" of the Bible and their significance for their lives.
ISBN 0-8254-3520-x **192 pp.** **paperback**

Bible Pinnacles
Over 80 detailed character sketches, pivotal incidents, miracles, and parables. Excellent homiletical helps.
ISBN 0-8254-3516-1 **192 pp.** **paperback**

Bible Promises
A look at the promises of the Bible and their significance to the believer.
ISBN 0-8254-3542-0 **192 pp.** **paperback**

Bible Windows
A rich collection of over 80 carefully chosen illustrations to better communicate the gospel message and bring to life the key points of its message.

ISBN 0-8254-3522-6   **180 pp.**   **paperback**

A Distinctively Different Commentaries Series. In an exciting, different style, Powell presents vivid illustrations and alliterative outlines which blend exposition and rich spiritual insight. Full of practical teaching and preaching helps.

Matthew's Majestic Gospel
ISBN 0-8254-3544-7   **526 pp.**   **paperback**

Mark's Superb Gospel
ISBN 0-8254-3510-2   **432 pp.**   **paperback**

Luke's Thrilling Gospel
ISBN 0-8254-3513-7   **508 pp.**   **hardcover**

John's Wonderful Gospel
ISBN 0-8254-3514-5   **446 pp.**   **hardcover**

The Amazing Acts
ISBN 0-8254-3545-5   **478 pp.**   **paperback**

The Exciting Epistle to the Ephesians
ISBN 0-8254-3537-4   **304 pp.**   **hardcover**

DAVID: His Life and Times
David, the "sweet psalmist of Israel," comes alive in a unique and refreshing manner, typical of Ivor Powell's writings. Provides a biographical commentary on David's life and times as well as devotional studies, outlines, and illustrations for teachers and preachers.

ISBN 0-8254-3532-3   **448 pp.**   **paperback**

What in the World Will Happen Next?
A scripturally-sound work which effectively describes the important prophetic events yet to be fulfilled. The book offers a wealth of material in the author's popular style on this fascinating and increasingly studied subject.

ISBN 0-8254-3524-2   **176 pp.**   **paperback**